Penny Silvers & Mary C. Shorey

Foreword by Linda K. Crafton

D1304626

Many Texts, Many Voices

Teaching Literacy and Social Justice to
Young Learners in the Digital Age

Stenhouse Publishers
Portland, Maine

Stenhouse Publishers
www.stenhouse.com

Credits
Pages 23 and 24: Figures 1.4 and 1.5 copyright 2007 by the National Council of Teachers of English. Reprinted with permission.
Page 127: Figure 5.3: Image courtesy of Library of Congress, Prints & Photographs Division, NYWT&S Collection, LC-USZ62-120210.

Library of Congress Cataloging-in-Publication Data
Silvers, Penny.
    Many texts, many voices : teaching literacy and social justice to young learners in the digital age / Penny Silvers and Mary C. Shorey ; foreword by Linda Crafton.
        p. cm.
    Includes bibliographical references and index.
    ISBN 978-1-57110-875-3 (pbk. : alk. paper) — ISBN 978-1-57110-965-1 (ebook)
    1. Language arts (Elementary)—Social aspects—United States. 2. Literacy—Social aspects—United States. 3. Social justice—Study and teaching (Elementary)—United States. 4. Children—Books and reading—United States. 5. Internet in education. I. Shorey, Mary C. II. Title.
    LB1576.S44 2012
    372.6—dc23
    2012002438

Cover design, interior design, and typesetting by Martha Drury
Manufactured in the United States of America

PRINTED ON 30% PCW
RECYCLED PAPER

18 17 16 15 14 13 12   9 8 7 6 5 4 3 2 1

Our book is dedicated to all the children and their caring teachers.

Contents

Foreword

I've often thought about how much courage it takes for a teacher to put herself out there—to open her classroom door and to display her teaching life for all to see. It is a scary thing to let others into your pedagogical heart and mind, but nothing much happens in our profession without teachers who are willing to scrutinize their instruction, their thinking, and their underlying beliefs.

I have rarely seen such inspired, organic teaching, learning, and inquiry as Penny and Mary so honestly describe in the pages of their ground-breaking book. No one can tell us how to teach; the most brilliant theorists and practitioners can only loosely highlight what works for them—and nothing works all of the time. One of the best things about this book is the way the authors define effective teaching by enticing us to explore compli-cated theories such as critical literacy and communities of practice, and then move into simple yet sophisticated learning stories that reveal the powerful structures and strategies that teachers can use to bring these ideas to life. Mary and Penny make clear that one of the crucial shifts that must occur in contemporary education is the move from teacher ideas to student passions connected to the social struggles that pepper the land-scape of our everyday lives.

New and experienced teachers alike will be drawn into these transforma-tive learning experiences enriched by children's conversations and Mary's teaching journal. As multiliteracies are defined and implemented in the pur-suit of social questions, it becomes easy to see that dialogic collaboration and community are the key processes by which we and our students improve.

Penny and Mary join a growing cohort of scholars who believe that teaching is indeed a political act. By using the twenty-first-century multimodal tools of learning, they show explicitly how teachers can bring curriculum to life by grounding the daily experiences of their students in authentic questions that thrill kids the most. These authors build on the classic work of Mary Cowhey and expand the contemporary thinking found in Jerry Harste and Vivian Vasquez's books on young children embracing a social justice way of caring, learning, and living.

With surprising speed, the twenty-first century has not only come upon us but is well under way. Surely we must be in a different place than we were decades ago when we started thinking about the value of teaching reading strategies versus the overemphasis on teaching reading skills. How have we progressed beyond the days of writing workshop and traditional literacy as the core of curriculum? In what ways have our views of students, ourselves, and the very purpose of education changed? In *Many Texts, Many Voices*, Penny Silvers and Mary Shorey answer these questions by posing their own significant inquiries during a period of more than five years. Through this book, they are not only *in* the twenty-first century, they *are* the new millennium.

Dr. Linda K. Crafton
February 2012

Acknowledgments

Writing this book has been an extraordinary journey, filled with unexpected experiences at every turn. We are so grateful for our colleagues, mentors, teachers, friends, parents, and the children who accompanied us and trusted us to tell their stories. As we've written, we've learned—and as we've learned, we've gained new insight and sustained passion to continue to advocate for the children and their teachers. We know how brilliant young children are, and how much they care about each other and the world. We know how much they love learning and how excited they are to work to make a difference. We also know—and have shown—that children become readers, writers, and communicators through the use of many different modalities and tools. They deserve the best that educators have to offer, and we hope that our continued work will contribute to an expanded perspective of literacy that embraces all the current insight about learning now and in the future. We also hope that our book contributes in some small way toward helping today's children become tomorrow's informed, caring, compassionate, articulate, well-educated citizens who understand what it means to live in a democracy. They are our future—we can't let them down.

Thanks to Pritchett School: Dr. Moreland, the principal; Dr. Jane Kier, former principal, colleague and friend; teachers Kathy Faierson, Heather Akiyoshi, Julie Pingel, and Patricia Eliopolous; volunteer "Grandma" Rhoda Maslov; parents Jeri Topel and Hara Ezell; and all the children. A special thank you to Jessie Topel, currently a fourth grader, whose participation in writing this book was inspirational; and to Mary's daughter, Natalie Vondrak, whose journey into teaching reminds us of the challenges and joys of becoming a professional educator. Thanks to our families, long suffering but always supportive and confident that our book will make a difference to children and teachers everywhere. Thanks to Earl, Penny's husband, for his constant encouragement and support; to Dr. Linda Crafton who started us on our journey; and to all our friends, mentors, and special colleagues who helped guide us into critical literacy. We also thank the Spencer Foundation for funding our initial research into early multiliteracies.

A very special thanks to Holly Holland, our magnificent editor, who recognized the importance of our story, helped us bring it to life, guided our work when we faltered, and never doubted that this book would be completed. We are grateful to Stenhouse for believing in us, for the excellence of their editorial and technical staff, and for their support all along the way.

Most of all, we thank you, the teachers, for reading our book. We hope the stories from Mary's classrooms will help you see possibilities for your students and their learning. We know the pressures you are under but we believe school can be more meaningful for children even as we implement standards, mandated curriculum, and required assessments. Critical literacy can help you fulfill curricular expectations while moving your students beyond the local and out into the world, learning and achieving more than you might have thought. Most of all, you will be helping children become critically literate from the start, providing them with the tools and confidence to make a positive difference as citizens of the world.

Introduction

Why is our story significant? How can this book support teachers in the challenging academic world we live in today? And, most important, how will this book make a difference for students? These are the questions we posed one September morning when we met at a public library to plan this book. After five years of researching, analyzing data and student work samples, watching videos, and meeting with students, we have so much to share and so much we want our teacher colleagues to know about early literacy development.

We each bring our own perspective to this collaborative writing process. Mary is a veteran teacher of grades one through four. Penny is both theorist and practitioner. A former reading specialist at Mary's school and now a university professor, Penny continues to work in classrooms and also researches in both urban and suburban locations. We have a long history of working together, coteaching in Mary's classroom, collaborating on literacy articles, and presenting at national and local conferences.

Our shared passion is making school meaningful and engaging for students. It is their story that needs to be told, and their voices will join with ours to tell you how much our youngest students are able to think, understand, and accomplish as they learn about the world, even as they are learning to read and write. They continually show us that they are capable of engaging in analytical and transformational work—from their first days of school.

We know you have students like Mary's in your classrooms: Sam, who feels more comfortable on a keyboard than using a pencil and paper to laboriously write a few sentences; Elizabeth, who sings and dances to a popular country song and makes connections between the lyrics and the book *The Rainbow Fish*; Raquel, who dramatizes her understanding of favorite books and uses drama and music to help her write poetry and stories; Jed, whose sophisticated writing reflects the many stories his parents shared with him before he could read on his own; and Arie, who calls himself a "citizen activist" and recruits his classmates to work on socially proactive projects such as a podcast about endangered animals.

An Expanded View of Literacy

When we started working together we didn't realize that literacy means so much more than being able to read and write print. The experiences of Mary's students engaging in literacy practices illustrate the ways that they use oral language, print, visual and digital tools, music, drama, and collaborative thinking to learn, care about others, and make a difference in the world. And as we applied our research about multiliteracies in Mary's classroom, we identified some significant core beliefs that we bring to life throughout the chapters in this book:

1. Literacy is expansive and complex. More than reading and writing print, multiliteracies include all the ways we can communicate in the twenty-first century.
2. Social participation within communities of practice lies at the heart of a multiliteracies classroom.
3. Young students bring background knowledge and experience with visual and digital tools into the classroom.
4. The rapidly expanding potential of technology suggests a more interactive, collaborative use of Internet resources.
5. A critical literacy perspective is necessary to successfully navigate our increasingly connected world.

Our book describes Mary's primary classrooms during the five years we researched early literacy development. When we started our collaboration, Mary had returned to teaching first grade after spending ten years in other elementary grade levels. As we completed our research in Mary's first-grade classroom, she moved up to third grade, where she currently teaches. Her school is located in a suburb northwest of Chicago. Once a predominantly homogeneous community, the demographics have changed in recent years. In a typical classroom at Mary's school one-third of the students are bilingual or multilingual and represent six or seven different cultures including Indian, Chinese, Korean, Japanese, Hispanic, Polish, and Russian. Students participate in English language learner (ELL) programs, and increasing numbers of students are recommended for RTI (Response to Intervention) services starting as early as kindergarten. All the teachers have at least a few special needs students in their classes. But regardless of the special needs, diversity, and demographics, we recognize that all students bring culturally rich and meaningful life experiences with them into the classroom. Many of Mary's students come from middle-class backgrounds where education is valued. We know that different communities present different sets of needs, but we believe that all students in all classrooms can—and must—learn to think and care about the world and each other.

Research Informs Practice

Our research into multiliteracies began when Linda Crafton, a university professor, colleague, and friend, asked to visit Mary's classroom and explore the topics of multiliteracies and critical literacy. Penny joined them soon after, and together we formed a professional study group. We used the communication tools of the twenty-first century to support our learning. Databases such as Questia, an online professional library, and professional organizations such as the International Reading Association (IRA) and the National Council of Teachers of English (NCTE) supplied us with continuous resources for professional learning.

Together we studied current research about "new literacies" and multiliteracies to broaden our understanding of early literacy practices. The first book we explored was *Multiliteracies: Literacy Learning and the Design of Social Futures* (Cope and Kalantzis 2000), which expands a traditional view of literacy to include digital literacy, visual literacy, and critical literacy. The authors suggest that an understanding of multiliteracies will help teachers recognize the need to provide their students with access to the language of work, power, and community and nurture the critical engagements necessary for students to design their social futures. Further research into critical literacy helped us understand that all texts and contexts can be examined for issues of power and privilege. As we deconstruct and reconstruct texts to make issues of power, oppression, diversity, and social justice more visible, we can find the impetus for taking some kind of social action (Vasquez et. al. 2004).

We then explored communities of practice, a model in which participants develop their identities and competencies through engaging in meaningful activities that move the whole community toward a shared goal (Wenger 1998). In the process of collaborating and constructing knowledge within the classroom community, all kinds and levels of participation are valued, and all the participants benefit from the shared experiences. We also found that Noddings's (1992) research on themes of care (caring for self, acquaintances, strangers, plants and animals, the Earth, human-made things, and ideas) supported critical literacy and these shared interactions within the community. Our multiliteracies research and observations in Mary's classroom confirmed the significance of literacy and learning as social practices and our understanding that language shapes thinking, while thinking is deepened through language (Halliday 1975).

Coming together from various perspectives, these related theories describe an interconnected relationship between different modes of expression (multimodal, multiliteracies). Each perspective or combination of perspectives reflects individual biases, beliefs, understandings, and intentions. We have learned that literacy is about communicating and conveying meaning through a variety of modalities for particular purposes. It involves engaging in meaningful activities with others in order to make the world a more just and caring place. Throughout the book, we reference these theories and show ways that they were instrumental in our learning and informed Mary's teaching. In the appendixes and references, we provide information for teachers, including an extensive bibliography of professional mentor resources and research for teachers who want to deepen their understanding of theory. We also include many of our favorite children's books and suggestions for thematic sets, along with various templates found in each chapter.

Merging these theories offers a way to retheorize or expand existing theories of early literacy development. If we begin at the local (classroom) level and then move into the community and beyond, we can plant the seeds of this expanded view of literacy. When students can live a critically caring life in a classroom that honors differences of all kinds and provides multimodal tools for exploring and learning about the world, there is the opportunity for transformation of self and community, and for making a difference in every aspect of life and living.

Students Inform Practice

Throughout our research, our own learning was messy and unpredictable. We often felt overwhelmed by the need to teach the required curriculum without a clear understanding of how to integrate multimodal tools or a critical literacy perspective. But as we took baby steps, and then giant steps, we also noticed more about what the children were really saying and doing as they met in small inquiry groups to pursue topics of interest. It quickly became clear to us that when the right structures and opportunities for purposeful learning were provided, young children could think and talk together about important social issues as they worked toward accomplishing shared learning goals. They were interested in a wide range of issues and able to understand important ideas that helped expand their awareness of the need to examine perspectives, consider alternate points of view, and take social action when necessary—but always in ways that were appropriate for young children.

Our research and collaborative teaching has helped us recognize that young children are definitely able to understand and explore complex issues that concern them and their world through many more modalities than print (Dyson 1993). A multiliteracies classroom should focus on community and social action, provide opportunities for students to learn and practice different ways of constructing and representing meaning, and enable them to explore identity and change. Through our guidance and support, Mary's students were changing from passively receiving information to actively constructing their own ideas and questioning ideas from different perspectives. Such a classroom also encourages students to analyze cultural trends and messages and become engaged, informed consumers and citizens (Bomer and Bomer 2001). They learn to use language purposefully and effectively in a variety of contexts (such as Facebook, Twitter, e-mail, texting, and G-chatting) and read and process information from different sources (visual, digital, and print).

But they also must learn to be cautious and aware as they investigate and communicate. Children today are bombarded with information. They need to understand that these "texts" have been written by authors (illustrators, web designers, and advertisers) who may have particular agendas, points of view, reasons, and intentions. While print is vitally important, we need to do more than help young learners decode words and answer simplistic comprehension questions about the stories in basal reading programs. These students need to become critical consumers as they learn how to use language and multiliteracies for their own purposes and needs. They also need to learn to ask critical questions that acknowledge different perspectives, rather than simply accepting a particular interpretation. As the children become more sensitive to how the media can position, condition, and persuade a consumer, reader, or media user, they will learn to rethink or reconstruct a new message or response and better understand that they can resist, change, or accept a particular point of view.

When we stepped back to really observe the children in Mary's classroom, we also saw that they were using a variety of strategies and tools to pursue meaningful inquiries *of their own*. At first, we didn't understand all the ways that her students were learning. Our observations helped us see that Mary's students were not just using music, art, dance, and drama to express their understanding of what they were reading and writing. These engagements in other modalities or sign systems were actually ways of comprehending and communicating meaning *in addition* to reading and writing.

Beneath the teacher's radar screen, a rich, learning-focused flurry of activity was going on, with children naturally gravitating together to pursue answers to questions that mattered to them. Even more revealing was the discovery that they were using the critical questions and reflective language that Mary purposefully modeled and shared in classroom read-alouds and lessons. The children were asking questions with minimal reinforcement from the teacher while they researched topics on the Internet; read about important subjects in books; examined and produced illustrations, graphics, slideshows, podcasts, wikis, and brochures; or discussed books from our guided reading time or during literature discussions. And they were finding their individual and collective voices as they learned to take some form of social action.

🌍 A Shared Vision

The following chapters present Mary's children engaging in meaningful experiences using all the tools available to them to explore, create, and collaborate. As authors, we have written our story with one voice, merging our perspectives, and at various times highlighting the point of view of the teacher, the researcher, and always the children. Through these stories, you will see how our understanding evolved and Mary's teaching changed as we learned more about the theories that informed our thinking and applied them in the classroom.

Each classroom experience revealed new and different possibilities leading us closer to a deeper understanding of the power and potential of a critically focused multiliteracies curriculum. We learned that multiliteracies are as complex as today's learners, and through our careful analysis and reflective research, we learned to "see" differently. As keen observers and students of our own practice, we took risks by questioning current teaching practices, designing critical curricular engagements, and moving forward with a commitment to take social action and to share this passion with the children.

Mary's students have shown us their capacity to care, to take social action, to inquire about important global issues, to use a variety of resources to communicate, and to learn together. When technology is available, they embrace it. When it is not available, they use whatever is provided—pencils, paper, markers, magazines, newspapers, novels, and textbooks. We believe that along with conventional print literacy, all children need time to explore topics of interest and importance, as well as opportunities to use other literacies and multimodal tools to expand their learning.

We invite you to join us in Mary's classroom and share our trials and triumphs through our exploration of multiliteracies and critical literacy. We hope the stories of her young students will reveal their capacity to move beyond the standard curriculum and use many different literacies to think globally and work together for a better world. We also hope that as you read and think about our experiences, you will envision ways to help your own students become critically literate from the start.

Chapter 1

Learning to Live Responsibly in a Critical Community of Practice

"Welcome to our classroom, Kiara," Mary announces, and in typical first-grade fashion the children gather around, excited to learn more about their new Japanese classmate. Although it is almost time for summer vacation, the students are still busy planning presentations and completing projects. At Mary's suggestion, they share the special things they like to do in Room 17. Without hesitation, students race to the classroom library and pull out some of their beloved books.

"Have you read the *Piggybook*?" asks Calvin. "It's one of our favorites."

"Look at the pictures," exclaims Lexie. "The boys turn into pigs!"

"So does everyone," adds Larry.

Mary interjects, "Do you remember why [author] Anthony Browne turns the dad and his sons into pigs?"

"Sure," Karen replies. "It's because it wasn't fair for the mom to do all the work. Dads and boys can do housework and cook, too." Not to be outdone by her friend Karen, Tori adds, "*Ruby's Wish* is my favorite. Did you know that Chinese girls couldn't go to the university a long time ago?"

Kiara smiles and shakes her head "no."

"We feel that boys and girls should have equal rights," Larry says, proudly using the vocabulary from a recent social studies unit.

"I like *Fly Away Home*," Zach says. "They just closed some of the homeless shelters in Chicago, and we are worried about that."

"We thought it might help to collect food for a food pantry," Brianna adds.

"It's our responsibility," says Kevin, demonstrating that he, too, recalls the focus of the first-grade social studies unit on citizenship and government.

"Can we tell Kiara about Grandma Ruth?" asks Karen.

Mary smiles and lets her students take charge of describing one of their most memorable critical literacy explorations from earlier in the school year.

🌍 Grandma Ruth

On a crisp winter afternoon, twenty-five first graders listen intently as Mary reads an article from the local newspaper to them. "Grandma Ruth," an elderly woman in their community, is being evicted from her house and being placed in a nursing home. Neighbors call her house an eyesore and insist that it be cleaned up or demolished. A developer is eager to build apartments on the property, and taxpayers seem to think this is an equitable arrangement. They consider it a way to salvage their property values by getting rid of this "wreck" of a house.

This story was a pivotal learning piece for Mary, Penny, and the students. Embedded in this real-life scenario were opportunities to involve students in actions, discussions, and reflections that could make a difference for others and themselves. By December, when this story emerged on the front page of the newspaper, Mary felt ready to address what she came to call a "tough issue" with her young learners. But this willingness to involve the children in taking a social action stance evolved slowly over the first months of school as we discussed and explored many ways to support and engage her students in meaningful literacy experiences.

Beginning to Learn About Multiliteracies

This first year of researching in Mary's classroom began with lots of questions and new insights about twenty-first-century learners. Mary had returned to teaching first grade after several years in other grades. She was anxious about covering everything in the required curriculum, working with a new team of teachers, helping her parent community understand the learning expectations for first grade, and meeting the needs of her diverse learners. She had just begun her doctoral studies but was not yet deeply informed about the theories that would guide her teaching and changing beliefs.

The term *multiliteracies* was new to all of us. As we explored all that it represented, we came to understand it as an expanded view of literacy that includes visual and digital literacies in addition to print. We knew that there are many ways, or modes, of making and understanding meaning. But rather than only thinking of literacy as reading and writing print, we needed to widen our definition of literacy to include a range of modalities such as music, drama, art, and technology. A deeper realization was that these modalities often overlap to convey meaning and build comprehension. Once we began to think about multiliteracies as a way of exploring the complex process of learning, we began to notice so much more in Mary's classroom. Children are always reading, singing, drawing, dancing, dramatizing, talking, and writing their way to understanding. These various literacies—or multiliteracies—validate what teachers intuitively understand: that learning to read, write, and comprehend our world involves more than scripted programs, drill and practice, and taking tests. Recognizing what students already know and do, capturing it, challenging it, and directly teaching through these different literacies becomes an authentic way to engage, enrich, and challenge today's young learners. It also provides opportunities to expand the curriculum and design meaningful ways to differentiate instruction.

Our professional community of practice (Wenger 1998) provided shared learning experiences for all of us—Mary, Penny, and Linda (our university colleague who worked with us during our first year in Mary's classroom). We met weekly and corresponded by e-mail, wrote notes together on Google Docs, and Skyped when we couldn't find a time to get together in person. Our professional community became a model for Mary as she developed her classroom community with a focus on social practices.

A New Capacity to Learn

Many of today's first graders know how to use a computer, and some have favorite Web sites. They may also participate in social networking sites specifically for children, such as Club Penguin. Because of the easy access to information through the media, they come to school exposed to so much and curious about so many things. Then again, first graders are always curious. They love to ask questions and explore. What's different these days is the amount of information that students have access to through digital resources and the media. Early on, we could easily see a need to help students synthesize this information and learn to recognize what is accurate and credible.

In her doctoral studies, Mary was learning about critical theory and the work of Paulo Freire, which provided the foundation for our under-standing of this literacy. Initially we weren't sure how to incorporate this in a primary classroom, but ultimately, critical literacy became the umbrella theory overarching all the literacies and a way to connect learning across subjects and content areas.

We define critical literacy as a perspective that examines and analyzes issues of power and privilege, and focuses on ways to redesign texts of all kinds (print, visual, and digital) for a more socially just world. It is a per-spective that values diversity and difference and helps students become consciously aware of ways that texts position them as readers. They also learn that there are many different kinds of texts in addition to print, such as illustrations, body language, Web pages, and screen images. Each "text" presents a particular point of view that can be analyzed and deconstructed, accepted or rejected. Students learn to "identify a text's origins and authority and examine how they are attempting to shape their values and beliefs" (Anstey and Bull 2006, 37).

The students also learn that as authors (including writers, illustrators, and Web designers) they have the power to create and convey messages to their readers that reflect a particular perspective or stance. Critical literacy requires that the reader/consumer examine multiple perspectives and ask, "Whose interests are being served?" and "Whose voice is heard—or silenced?" Rather than an addition to a lesson or curriculum, critical lit-eracy is a way of thinking, communicating, analyzing, and living a literate life. Critical literacy also implies the possibility of taking some kind of social action in order to support a belief, make a difference, or simply help during a time of need. The more we thought about and read about critical literacy, the more this way of thinking became an integral part of Mary's curriculum and instruction.

Examining Social Issues

Early in our first year of working together, we saw an opportunity for introducing more critically focused instruction. After an interactive class read-aloud of *Piggybook* by Anthony Browne, Mary's students surprised us with a heated discussion about gender roles. In *Piggybook* (1986), Browne challenges gender stereotypes. At one point the mother tells her husband and two sons that they are "pigs" because the house is such a mess. When she leaves, a remarkable physical transformation occurs in which dad and the boys actually turn into real pigs. Over time, they realize that they should be part of the cleanup squad at home, and as they take on more domestic roles, they regain their human forms. Mom returns and all is well with everyone helping each other do all the domestic tasks.

During read-aloud time, Mary tries to choose books with particular social issues and themes that support her social studies units, such as this one about families. Her simple questions to the class ("What do moms do? What do dads do?") turned into a lively discussion about how a mother's role is to work, cook, clean, take care of the kids and of how dads work, barbecue (only), play sports, and take business trips.

"Well, I think that the mom should be mad; those boys are pigs!" Jenny observed.

"I think it is funny, Kevin said. "Look at all the pigs in the pictures. They are everywhere."

"Notice how tired the mom looks; she has to do all the work," Mary added. "Did you notice how the dad and her sons order her around? What do you think about that?"

"Well, I think the dad is probably tired too. He has to go to work every day," Larry responded.

"So does the mom! And she has to do housework, too," Karen retorted.

"Yes, she does the cooking and the cleaning and everything!" Jody said.

"Well, my dad cooks. He barbeques the best burgers," argued Jason.

"It is the mom's job to take care of the house, and the boys have school-work," added Eric.

Mary let the children comment for a few minutes and then tried to summarize their thinking. "Hmm, I'm hearing that moms and dads have different roles," she said. "Let's talk about that."

To broaden the students' stereotypical ideas about gender, Mary set up opportunities for her students to look through magazine pictures and books in the classroom library to see what roles were typically given to the boys and men, versus the girls and women. One group of students decided to take a survey of the class, asking students what they wanted to be when they grew up, and then they graphed the results on the computer. They used their data to show categories of jobs and discuss how gender roles reflected the beliefs of the class.

Figure 1.1

WHAT ARE TEXT SETS?

A text set is a collection of resources that are grouped together to support a topic, genre, or author study. This collection includes fiction and nonfiction books of various reading levels that are selected to support a range of experiences and interests. A text set can include charts and maps, poetry and songs, photographs, almanacs, or encyclopedias. Digital resources, such as student-friendly search engines and bookmarked (previewed) Web sites, should also be part of text sets.

To capture the students' enthusiasm as they examined and discussed their views, Mary played a country song titled, "Mr. Mom" (Lonestar 2004). Students danced and sang along with the lively music and lyrics that challenge traditional gender roles. Julian shared that his father was a stay-at-home dad, and the children marveled at this and told him that it was so "cool." Some of the students dramatized different parent roles, and others initiated a reader's theater center.

With our heightened awareness of questioning from a critical perspective, Mary was able to expand the students' beliefs about gender roles into an exploration of stereotypes of all kinds, including grandparents, sports, and multicultural issues prevalent in her classroom. We also discovered that the children wanted to see themselves and their families represented in the books Mary was reading to them. With the help of the school librarian, she developed text sets (see Figure 1.1) and brought in many multicultural books for the children to examine. Exploring gender roles in different cultures during read-aloud time became a focus for further study and discussion.

Reading and Questioning

The children loved read-aloud time in Mary's room. It was a special time for group discussions and sharing of ideas. Mary would purposefully ask questions and validate student responses as she guided them to deeper understandings, encouraging critical questions about both the pictures and words. Typically, Mary used think-alouds to focus primarily on vocabulary, word choice, and ways the authors used written text to create mental images. But recognizing that visual literacy is an important component of meaning making, Mary began guiding the children to carefully examine the illustrations in the picture books she was reading to them. She highlighted the idea that images could be used to construct and convey

Figure 1.2

CRITICAL QUESTIONS

- Whose voices are heard? Whose voices are absent?
- What does the author/illustrator want the reader to think/understand?
- What is an alternative to the author/illustrator's message?
- How will a critical reading of this text help me change my views or actions in relation to other people?

meaning, in the same way that words are used to help the reader comprehend a written text. She consistently emphasized that the pictures were texts that we could "read" as well as words. Sometimes the images supported the text, and sometimes they would tell their own story. Mary talked about the illustrator as well as the author of each book, so the children became familiar with both roles. Students began to understand that images are designed by the illustrator for particular reasons and are as important to a good book as the words chosen by the author. Highlighting both print and images provided an added dimension to book discussions and helped the children recognize how important both were to the meaning of the story. It also helped make a smooth transition to asking critically focused questions.

Taking a cue from some of our professional reading, we decided to use four core questions to help students focus on thinking from a critical perspective (Vasquez 2004). Mary posted these questions in the classroom as an anchor chart and used it repeatedly during read-alouds and class discussion about books or projects being studied (see Figure 1.2 and Appendix A).

Understanding Critical Literacy

From the work of Comber, Harste, and others, we know that literacy is a unique reflection of each individual. Our personal literacy and identity represent all our prior knowledge and life experiences within various social, cultural, and political contexts. We wanted to make sure that the students understood that authors, illustrators, or Web designers always have a particular perspective or point of view—whether it is reflected in a piece of writing, a picture, or a digital message or Web site. We also considered it important for students to recognize that, as readers, they too have specific perspectives and that their comprehension is informed by their unique backgrounds and life experiences. We wanted them to learn that readers can accept or reject the messages conveyed by an author and they have the power to rewrite that message or recreate it in a different way. A more complex idea for the children to understand was the notion that there can be many "right answers" depending upon different points of view. A reader can ask a range of important questions when interpreting a text and consider many different "answers" or solutions.

This was a lot to think about, and Mary was enthusiastic but hesitant about embracing these dimensions of critical literacy. Never losing sight of what would be best for her students, she repeatedly asked, "What does this look like in first grade?" We all wondered about the appropriateness of addressing critical issues such as race, war, homelessness, and gender with her young students. Indeed, one of her first-grade colleagues was adamant that young children must be sheltered from the problems of the world, stating that, "First grade should be happy, safe, and fun, and those topics are not fun."

We, too, wanted the students to read books that were enjoyable and study topics that would enrich—but not disturb them emotionally. But some of the issues we wanted to explore were already part of the existing curriculum, including the environment, endangered species, needs and wants, multicultural families, and diverse communities. The challenge was figuring out how to include reflective thinking and analytical questioning in everyday events and then finding ways to introduce a critical literacy perspective where it seemed appropriate. We wanted to help students learn to critique, but not always criticize; to question, but also consider different points of view; and to accept and value differences as a way of being a responsible citizen—in the classroom and outside of school as well. A very real concern was how to accomplish all the testing, teaching, and academic requirements if another layer (critical literacy) was added to an already packed curriculum. It all seemed very complicated and overwhelming.

But we persevered, and as we slowly added a critical dimension to the required curriculum, Mary's journals helped us focus on classroom issues and applications.

10–6 Initial wonderings:
Critical literacy—what does it mean?
My first thoughts remind me of how impressionable early learners are and cause me to pause and think about how important it is to observe and support children as they question, examine, and put their own ideas into place about the world.

I believe my teaching involves honoring all perspectives and helping children to look beyond the surface. So much of what early literacy looks like *to me is prescriptive and drill. We are told to group students according to their needs, but I wonder how we are really determining their needs. I'm thinking of Zack today and the grin on his face when I acknowledged his great scientific thinking and his ability as an artist . . . what an obligation the teacher has. With a simple comment I can impact identity and effect change . . .*

I need to use my "power" carefully and look for ways to empower my students. I need to help them to accept the challenges of living in a world very different than the one I grew up in, a world where they need to be problem solvers, thinkers, and creative individuals.

<u>10–24 worries</u>
How can I balance the "how-to" . . . or "cracking the code" with this focus on critical literacy? Can I trust that it will just happen? In curriculum that emphasizes data–based decision making, how will this play out? What is all the testing data really showing us? Don't we learn even more by informed observations as good "kid–watchers"?

My first thoughts are about how to make my centers focus more on critical literacy. But then my next thought is that perhaps the centers should be places where students practice skills like grammar and spelling. I know that I shouldn't separate or isolate them, but I'm worried that my students will "miss" something.

As we worked with Mary's students, we could see that they were really excited about discussing real-world issues, and they knew a lot from popular news media sources. Her early reservations about critical literacy with young children also began to slowly fade as she actively explored critical pedagogy in her doctoral studies and observed her students' interest and enthusiasm for learning about current events and critical incidents in the world beyond school. Recognizing that authenticity is a key part of engagement and that children are inevitably exposed to tough issues through the media, we all thought that a safe classroom setting might be an ideal place to address tough social issues.

From research about how the brain learns, we found that "basic components of social responsibility such as empathy, moral sensibilities, the understanding of social conventions, and political awareness emerge prior to the age of eight" (Berman 1997, 22). We discovered that young children could demonstrate moral reasoning and compassion and could understand different perspectives. We also found that it is often the unknown or misconceptions that can be most worrisome to children. Through our professional reading and close observations of the children engaged in exciting work, we became convinced that a critical literacy focus was not only advantageous for students, but also obligatory for twenty-first-century learning.

Our thinking was to expand the required curriculum to include some kind of critical component that would enhance and deepen the students' understanding of various subjects and topics rather than adding new content to the existing curriculum. From the kinds of conversations Mary's students were having and the books they were choosing to read, we knew they were thinking creatively and making important connections with their own lives and ideas. A tool that helped Mary broaden her literacy focus and expand the language arts curriculum, district mandates, and state standards was Luke and Freebody's Four Resources model (1999), which we adapted to create a more critically focused curriculum (see Figure 1.3 and Appendix B).

Figure 1.3

EXPANDED FOUR RESOURCES MODEL		
	Conventional Curriculum	**Expanded Critical Curriculum**
Code Breaker	• alphabetic principle • sounds in words • spelling • grammar conventions	• learn about a variety of ways to talk and behave that are unique to cultures, situations, and organizations
Meaning-Maker	• vocabulary instruction • strategy instruction (i.e., predicting, inferring, synthesizing) • compose text (written, oral, visual, or digital)	• tap into student's background knowledge, culture, native language, or prior experiences
Text User	• read and write different genres (fiction, nonfiction, poetry)	• explore purposes of texts and multimodal forms of expression, subtle meanings, hidden messages in words, images, Web sites
Text Analyst (Critic)	• examine author's purpose • engage multiple perspectives	• ask critical questions • act on understandings

Adapted from Luke and Freebody 1999

For example, when Mary discussed the district focus on phonemic awareness, phonics, and fluency, she referred to **code breaking**, which includes all the alphabetic principles, sounds in words, spelling, and grammar conventions. But this category can also be expanded to include learning about a variety of ways to talk and behave that are unique to different cultures, situations, and organizations (such as school).

Meaning making is about vocabulary and comprehension and involves composing and constructing meaning with written, visual, digital, and oral language. But it also requires us to consider a student's background knowledge, culture, native language, or prior experiences in order to communicate effectively.

The **text user** category supports a traditional focus on reading and writing different genres (fiction, nonfiction, poetry). It also highlights using texts for various purposes and in various contexts (whether print, images, or digital information).

Finally, the category of **text analyst (critic)** suggests that texts represent points of view, that they are socially constructed or authored by someone with a particular perspective that can be accepted or rejected by the reader and reconstructed for a different meaning or purpose. This category supports our focus on critical literacy and multimodal expression.

Moving into critical literacy involved some risk taking as a teacher. Mary describes herself as a constructivist teacher who looks for ways to empower students and follow their leads, but her emerging critical literacy focus involved more. We recognized that it wasn't enough just to design an authentic curriculum and provide books with social issues for the children to read. Mary also intentionally looked for ways to demonstrate that learning can make a difference not only in the classroom, but beyond. Her earliest questions, influenced by Noddings's work, were "Is it enough to care?" and "What does it really mean to care?" The children logically explained that you take care of people you like or love. But we wanted them to understand that care also implies action on behalf of someone or something: to take a stand, to resist, to protect, or to protest when an injustice occurs.

Mary started to look for appropriate opportunities to raise the students' critical awareness. Her instruction became more purposeful as we recognized that it was not enough to simply see or notice possibilities for critical engagements without also taking some kind of social action whenever possible. In December of our first year of working together, Grandma Ruth provided a natural connection that became a transformational learning experience for everyone.

Social Responsibility

The children were sitting right in front of Mary as she read a newspaper article to them about an elderly woman being evicted from her house. Suddenly there was a loud gasp as first grader Karen caught the headline and shouted out, "Does that really say 'They Can Kill Me First'? What does that mean?" she asked. The children were instantly engaged and discussed the picture, the headline, and the news story with Mary, wondering how something like this could be allowed to happen.

Before Mary introduced this newspaper article to her first graders, she brought it to our professional community of practice and wondered if it was appropriate. She was beginning a social studies unit on government that included learning about being a responsible citizen. Students had just been introduced to the term *democracy* and the values that form a democratic system, including love of liberty and respect for individual rights. These ideas seemed to be embedded in this newspaper article. We thought our previous work raising critical questions from different points of view and posing problems to young children had laid the foundation for understanding this article. So we forged ahead.

Mary discussed the cover photo in which the wrinkled, elderly face of Grandma Ruth stared defiantly at the reader from the center of the page. We referred to this kind of picture as a "demand image"[1] and talked about how the photographer used it to pull us in and establish a relationship with the person in the picture. As the children discussed the powerful headline, the conversation shifted to word choice and how the author also demanded the reader's attention by quoting "they can kill me first." Mary reread the article to the children several times, and everyone decided that those compelling words together with the intense picture captured the readers' interest and helped them understand the strong message of the article. Further conversation reinforced the idea that we "read" both words and images and that they each convey a particular message that helps us comprehend more deeply.

"I think that the newspaper wanted us to see what this lady looks like," Tori said. "It's a big photo."

"She looks old and sad," Kevin agreed.

"She is supposed to," Larry said, and the others turned to look at him.

"What do you mean?" Mary asked.

---

1. We use this term to refer to ways in which photographers, Web designers, illustrators, and others position pictures or photos to encourage reader and viewer response. In this case, the intention of using the picture of Grandma Ruth was to "demand" that the reader look directly at the woman's face and feel her pain and concern.

"Well, the photographer wants us to understand how she feels," Larry added.

Mary continued, "Hmm, I believe that the reporter and the photographer *did* choose this photo on purpose. I'm wondering why it is on the front page of the paper, and also why it is being reported now, in December? Turn and talk to a partner about this."

After a few minutes, Mary called the whole group back together, and Karen raised her hand to speak. "I think December is when we celebrate Christmas, and it would be sad to not be in your house at Christmas."

"Or Hanukkah," Lexie commented, "I celebrate Hanukkah."

"I feel sorry for her," Calvin said, and his classmates followed with a chorus of, "Me, too."

"Did anybody talk about why it is on the front page?" asked Mary.

Jodie raised her hand and said, "We did. We think it is the most important page."

Mary continued, "Yes, authors, photographers, and reporters all intentionally choose their words, their messages, pictures, and the placement of all of these as they design their story. I agree with you. By putting this photo on the front page, it helps us as readers to feel sorry for this old woman."

The students next examined a smaller photo of this woman's house in the same article. Some thought it didn't look so bad while others believed it was really awful. They wondered out loud why that particular photo of her house had been chosen. The caption used the expression *eyesore*, and the students felt that this choice of words was powerful. They also noticed that the article referred to the woman as "Grandma Ruth." We talked about the feelings that the word *grandma* evokes and how the author of the article wanted people to establish a personal and emotional connection with this woman to reinforce feeling sorry for her.

The students loved acting out stories and thought using this kind of process drama would help them to better understand Grandma Ruth's plight. The article said that at one point Grandma Ruth had been moved to a nursing home but that she had escaped from this placement and returned to her home. This description became an action scene in the students' dramatic interpretation. It sounded something like this:

Policewoman (Jodie): You must return to the nursing home.
Grandma Ruth (Tori—grabbing a scarf to tie on her head and speaking in a shaky voice that she thought sounded "old"): I have lived here my whole life. I don't want to move.

Policeman (Kevin): You will be safe at the nursing home.
Grandma Ruth: NO! I WANT MY OWN HOME!
Neighbor 1 (Sam): . . . but it is an eyesore.
Neighbor 2 (Daniel): It belongs to her.
Citizen 1 (Elizabeth): Maybe we can help her to keep it. We can clean it up.

Students put their language to her actions and connected strongly with her dilemma. They took turns playing her part and the part of the neighbors. As students assumed these different roles, they became more deeply involved, and when a follow-up article ran two weeks later, students could hardly wait to continue their discussions.

The second article said that she would be allowed to remain in her home a little longer until the judge decided what to do with her, and then it offered a possible solution. A local builder wanted to develop Grandma Ruth's land. He would build a new home for her and would also build a few other homes on her land. This seemed to be a good solution, but there were new critical questions to ask.

In the new photograph, Grandma Ruth looked different. She was standing in a room of her house, looking around at her belongings. This time, her situation didn't seem so dire. Mary helped the children ask:

() Why did they choose this particular photograph?
() What does the headline suggest to the reader?
() Whose voice is being heard and whose is not?
() Is this a good solution for Grandma Ruth?
() Who stands to gain from this solution? Why?

Discussions focused on the idea that Grandma Ruth would be given a new home. As everyone began to think about this solution, Jodie's hand shot up, and she said, "But Grandma Ruth doesn't want a new home." Immediately other hands went up: "She wants her old one." "Can't she just fix it up?" "Maybe we can help her clean it up." Brianna's response was the most creative: "Maybe she can go on *Extreme Makeover*!" "Good idea," was the class response. The discussion continued until Karen said, "I think Grandma Ruth should have a choice." "Yes," replied Larry, "it is her land." And Kevin said, "It isn't fair."

Messages of Care and a Call for Action
The children were able to see that Grandma Ruth's voice was being silenced. They couldn't understand why a builder would build on land that belonged

to her and not pay her for it. Class discussions focused on ways to support Grandma Ruth, and the definition of *care* expanded beyond caring about Grandma Ruth as a person to caring about freedom and choice and taking social action. Students shared their responses with each other and decided that together they could provide a strong message of support.

Mary asked the children to consider how they could communicate their opinions as citizens. She suggested that they share their thoughts with Grandma Ruth and write to the newspaper. They heard and responded to Kevin's words, "We love Grandma Ruth, and we care," and the students enthusiastically created multimodal messages. Sammy drew a picture and wrote his thoughts on the computer. Kevin's message was in picture form with Christmas lights drawn on Grandma Ruth's home to make her feel "warm and happy." And Elizabeth voiced her opinion in strong, bold print with simple and powerful words: "Grandma Ruth should have a choice!"

To make their views more personal, Mary scanned the students' pictures and writings, took digital photos, and linked them all together in a slideshow that she sent directly to the reporter/author of the articles (see Figures 1.4 and 1.5 for examples).

Two weeks later the class received a response from the newspaper thanking them for their messages. The reporter also reassured everyone

Figure 1.4
Karen's Opinion About Grandma Ruth's Predicament

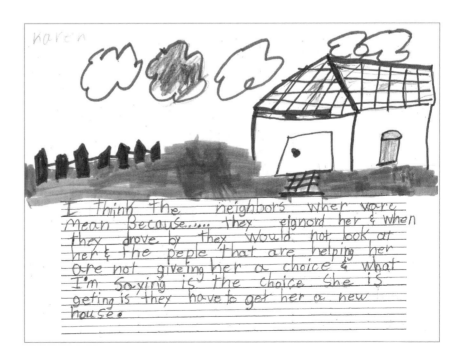

Figure 1.5
Ivan's Plan for
Helping Grandma
Ruth

Let her kepe it or give the mony to her. The
Gevmet said to rek it. Pipoale shode hlp her.

that Grandma Ruth had received the class messages of care and acknowledged that the students were exercising their rights and responsibilities as
good citizens. The letter included a publication date for a follow-up article
that would reveal the judge's decision and an e-mail address for further
correspondence with the reporter. On the last day of school, Mary and her
students received this letter from Grandma Ruth:

Dear Ms. S.,
I thank you very much for being such a wonderful teacher,
teaching your young Kings and Queens to love and care for
others. It was a wonderful letter I received from you and your
Kings and Queens through the newspaper.
    To the Kings and Queens you are teaching, let them know that
I appreciate their caring about Grandma Ruth and that I am fine
and still fighting the people that want to take my home away from
me.
    You see I had wonderful teachers, like yours, and it has carried
me through life's journeys, so keep learning and always be honest
to yourself and others and you will get to age 83 with much love
and caring. May Blessings be with you always.

With all my love,
Thank-you,
Grandma Ruth M.

P.S. I have kept all your sent papers, close to my heart.

Figure 1.6
Researching and
Learning Together

Participation in Communities of Practice

This authentic learning experience focusing on Grandma Ruth gave the students a chance to dig into their required social studies unit about the rights and responsibilities of citizens. They used multiliteracies resources (print, digital, visual) to understand Grandma Ruth's story and express their opinions. More importantly, the students began to come together as a community of practice.

The students were united in wanting a positive outcome for Grandma Ruth. Together they brainstormed ideas of ways to help. Together they divided the work of designing their responses, putting their individual ideas into one strong message of hope and support (see Figure 1.6). And together they used words and images to craft a message for Grandma Ruth that they sent back to the reporter. Ultimately, their collaborative work led to their taking a proactive stance and engaging in appropriate—but powerful—social action. Grandma Ruth's letter to them on the last day of school confirmed the significance of their work and validated their concern and commitment to help. Important work for a first-grade community of practice! And they learned in a very authentic way about citizenship and democracy by living it in their classroom.

PARTICIPATION IN COMMUNITIES OF PRACTICE			
Developing Routines	**Using Multiliteracies Resources**	**Comprehension and Expression Through Different Modalities**	**Taking Action**
• Offering choices • Asking critical questions • Exploring perspectives	• **Print** (books, newspapers) • **Digital** (search engines, Web sites) • **Visual** (photos, artwork, graphic organizers) • **Other** (music, drama)	• Writing • Artwork • E-mail • Slideshows • Photographs • Skits • Podcasts • Video	• Correspondence with news reporter • Messages of care and a call for action and justice

Figure 1.7

The Grandma Ruth experience and all the other applications of critical literacy in Mary's classroom were the real "tests" of its applicability and value. We watched the children working together to solve important problems, designing products to show their learning, engaging in complex thinking and collaboration, and taking meaningful action to make a difference for Grandma Ruth. Throughout all these learning experiences, the children used a variety of multimodal tools and media to find answers to their questions (see Figure 1.7). The constant was a focus on community with an emphasis on social justice and critical literacy. This realization led us to develop a multiliteracies framework that represents and supports our vision of twenty-first-century literacy development.

A Multiliteracies Framework

Our Multiliteracies Framework (Figure 1.8 and Appendix C) has two major components. The first consists of three nested circles within the learning cycle. The center circle, or core, represents critical literacy and highlights the need for every learning experience to consider different perspectives, value and honor difference, and take appropriate social action whenever possible. The second circle focuses on social practices, highlighting the social nature of learning as a dialogic, interactive process. The third circle presents the idea that learning is multimodal and that we use a variety and combination of tools to construct and communicate meaning.

Figure 1.8
Multiliteracies
Framework

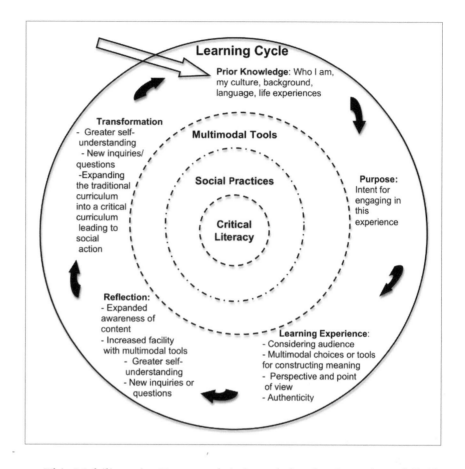

This Multiliteracies Framework is intended to be dynamic and fluid. The three inner circles illustrate the ways that critical literacy, social practices, and multimodal tools are used for inquiries and communication. These are embedded in all parts of the learning cycle across the curriculum. The dotted lines of the model represent movement across and within the cycles leading, ultimately, to transformation using any or all of the multiliteracies and available multimodal tools.

The outer circle is called the Learning Cycle. It is adapted from the Inquiry Based Evaluation Model that was developed some years ago (Crafton 1991). Students always bring their **prior knowledge** to any learning experience, and these unique perspectives shape their understanding of what is being investigated or studied. As the learning cycle evolves, students **consider their purpose** or intent for doing this work, **engage in the inquiry**, and then **reflect on their learning**. Throughout the cycle, students work within small groups or communities of practice and interact in meaningful ways with different people, texts, or contexts. These contexts are as varied as the multimodal tools used to explore their inquiries. They can include face-to-face small- or large-group work, virtual digital experiences, Internet research, primary source investigations, and more.

During the learning cycle, participants talk and think together, share ideas, exchange points of view, and gain new insights. In fact, unlike our older notions of learning as a solo experience, today's learning is an active process that depends on opportunities to talk, work, and think together with others. Finally, reflecting on their new understanding with other learners provides the potential for change and **transformation**. Sometimes this change is huge; really transforming thinking and behavior, helping the learner become more aware of social issues and making a difference. For example, this was the case when the children began to explore gender issues with *Piggybook*, and some of them changed their ideas about gender roles and the importance of being strong females. Other times it may simply lead to more questions and even new inquiries. At all times, students are learning to make appropriate choices, taking responsibility for their work, and gaining new insights as they move toward a more informed, inclusive, expansive view of the world.

Through reflection on their experiences and shared understanding, new questions emerge and the inquiry or learning cycle begins again. Each time students enter into this cycle, their insights and understanding are broader, deeper, and more informed. The process continues as long as interest is sustained and students' inquiries lead them toward taking some kind of social action.

Social Participation: The Work of a Critical Community of Practice

"What else can we share about our class with Kiara?" Mary asks her students. "Why don't we talk about all of us in our classroom community?"

"Well, Sam is our computer expert. If you have a question, he is the one to ask. Our teacher asks him questions, too," Calvin says with a smile.

"And I am a music expert," Elizabeth says.

"I am a sports expert," adds Kevin.

"And I know a lot about dogs," continues Brianna.

"And now we need to add Kiara to our expert chart," Tori interjects, referring to a class expert chart posted on the wall (see Figure 1.9).

"Good idea," Mary replies, "I wonder if you could also describe the ways that we learn together as a class. What did we learn from our experi-

Class Experts

Aidan	Computer
Mark	Reading
Sindhu	Math (multiplication/division)
Lauren	
Josh	
Daniel	power point
Jared E.	Technology
Carson	Minecraft
Tyler	Basketball
Jared H.	Greek Mythology
Haeyun	Drawing
Grace	Dancing 3 Singing 2
Tiffany	Playing & swimming and acting
Mindy	Dancing
Julian	Fixing computer animation
Sabrina	Reading
Michelle	Reading
Kate	The Green Bay Packers
Jin	running
David	Minecraft
Leah	Writing Stories 'N sports
Cassandra	Sports and Art
Ariella	Dance Shows
Amira	Figure Skating and Singing
Casey	Fixing Computer Issues

Figure 1.9 Expert Chart

Figure 1.10 A Community That Cares

ence with Grandma Ruth? What do we learn when we have class meetings or work in interest groups?"

"Well, we know that together is better," Karen says, thoughtfully. "When we listen and share ideas with each other, we all feel good."

Allen adds, "And we learn more. My mom always says, 'Two heads are better than one.'"

"We call ourselves a 'community that cares,'" Larry replies, pointing to a sticky note attached to the phone. "When we answer the phone, we always say, 'Room 17, a community that cares.'"

Mary continues, "Yes, you all are right. We are a community that cares. We care in big ways and in little ways. When we learned about Grandma Ruth, we wrote to the newspaper and sent messages of care. A few weeks ago we cleaned up the playground, throwing litter away and demonstrating that we care about our school and the environment. We also show how much we care every day by respecting each other and celebrating our differences. We use that expert chart and share our talents. We are always looking for ways to use our learning to make a positive difference for others and ourselves" (see Figure 1.10).

Insights & Emerging Understandings

Initially, we thought that each critical literacy experience had to become a big unit. Then we began to understand that opportunities for critical work are embedded in everyday life in the classroom. Young students can learn to critique a text and analyze and explore meaning from different perspectives. There is a natural connection between learning the conventions of reading and writing and learning to think about each other and the world. Without an understanding of literacy practices as social, critical, and multimodal, comprehension becomes flat and two-dimensional in a three-dimensional world. We believe it is our obligation to help young students recognize multiple perspectives, consider alternative points of view, and understand that their actions and involvement in social issues can help make the world safer and more accepting of difference and diversity. And as they are immersed in meaningful learning experiences, they are also developing and refining their literacy skills—reading, writing, listening, speaking, drawing, creating digital images, using digital media, dancing, singing, and connecting with others across languages and cultures—to become a classroom community of practice.

Suggestions for creating a critical classroom community:

() Start with teacher read-alouds that address critical literacy topics. Intentionally use read-aloud and think-aloud time to make your own thoughts about the text or images visible to the students. This is the time to start asking and discussing critical questions.

() Create an anchor chart of Critical Questions. As children become familiar with these questions, refer to this chart across all content areas.

() Put together a set of books, articles, magazines, Web sites, and related resources on subjects or topics that have particular meaning to the class, or are related to critical incidents (such as family, current events or stories your class has discussed or become involved in, or other local events of importance in your school or classroom).

() Encourage your students to think and talk about social issues, and look for ways to encourage discussions that might lead to further inquiries (such as gender or the environment) as well as connect to the mandated curriculum.

() Establish classroom communities of practice that support all levels of participation. Help students understand that to care means respecting each other, being good citizens, and using learning to make a difference for others and themselves.

( ) Encourage the use of many different multimodal tools to explore student inquiries and share understanding. Set up centers or work stations where students have access to a variety of materials including print resources, drawing materials, computers, and iPads (if available).

( ) Remember that children naturally use multiliteracies to learn about their world. Our job is to teach them strategies for using these tools, interpreting information from different points of view, and learning to talk and collaborate together to accomplish important goals and to take social action. This is the heart of the Common Core State Standards and more.

Favorite Books with Critical Potential: Family, Gender, and Identity
(See Appendixes T and V for more text suggestions.)
Amazing Grace by M. Hoffman
Boy, Can He Dance! by E. Spinelli
Chrysanthemum by K. Henkes
Hooway for Wodney Wat by H. Lester
Koala Lou by M. Fox
Little Granny Quarterback by B. Martin Jr. and M. Sampson
My Great-Aunt Arizona by G. Houston
Oliver Button Is a Sissy by T. DePaola
The Paper Bag Princess by R. Munsch
Piggybook by A. Browne
Players in Pigtails by S. Corey
The Rainbow Fish by M. Pfister
Ruby's Wish by S. Y. Bridges
William's Doll by C. Zolotow

Chapter 2

Hurricane Katrina: Adding a Critical Dimension to the Curriculum

"Did you hear about the hurricane?" asked Blake.

"Yes, it was a really big one that hit New Orleans. I saw pictures on the news!" Becca exclaimed.

"It looks so scary. I hope we don't have one here," Felicia said.

"Oh, we can't," Blake assured her. "Hurricanes only happen near oceans."

Becca was still disturbed by the events, "But so many people got flooded, and they have nowhere to go."

"Well, I'm researching it right now, and I'll have more information soon," Blake said confidently, sounding more like a veteran journalist than a six-year-old.

Hurricane Katrina hit New Orleans in August 2005, at the beginning of our school year. The disaster was featured on the television news almost constantly, and Mary's first graders were both horrified and fascinated by the destructive power of the storm and the scientific information shared on the news channels and the Internet. Like people all over the country, we were riveted by the stories of tragedy, heroism, and loss. But as we studied and reflected on the aftermath of the hurricane, we also discovered new

ways to bring a critical perspective to current events and to link these
issues to the curriculum.

A Critical Community of Practice

In the second year of our collaboration, we wanted to create a community
of practice in the classroom, which Wenger (1998) describes as inquiry
that is shaped by the shared interests and work of the group. As members
accomplish the group's tasks, they gain individual insights but also expand
their thinking collectively. We learned with the Grandma Ruth project the
previous year that when students work together toward a common goal or
focus on a shared purpose, all the participants are changed in positive
ways. We wanted the class to continue collaborating, reflecting on their
learning, and valuing each other's unique talents, interests, and expertise.
From the first day of school, we planned to celebrate diversity and build a
culture of caring—for each other and for the world beyond school.

Through our reading and studying, we realized that by adding a critical dimension to the concept of caring, we could move beyond purely
emotional connections to thoughtful activism and problem solving. Penny
summed up our thinking in a journal entry:

> *Our understanding of critical theory helps us better understand issues of
> relationships, power, equity, justice, and equal access. As "caring" teachers, it
> is our obligation to recognize exclusion in whatever form and work to change
> it. This includes learning to hear and see from a critical perspective and
> demonstrating this for the students by the words we use and by our actions.*

Rather than just a feeling of fondness for others, we believe that *caring*
has to be redefined as a commitment to consider different points of view,
recognize stereotypical behaviors and attitudes, and work toward inclu-
siveness. For Mary this translated into an intentional focus on instruction
that reflected diversity and supported strong relationships.

Like most teachers, Mary has some favorite start-up activities. In previous years she had the students play "getting to know each other" games.
This year, however, the focus became more than just getting acquainted.
She designed lessons that celebrated the diversity in her classroom and
emphasized activities that would last beyond the first week or two of
school. An important step was collecting text sets of multicultural books
that reflected the ethnicities of Mary's students, including Russian,

---

FAMILY HISTORY SURVEY

Family name _____

Dear Families,

    We are learning about each other and celebrating the many ways that we are alike and different. Please help your student fill out this brief survey. Please return by _____. Students will share these with their classmates. Thank you!

What country(ies) did our family immigrate from?

What are some of our family favorites?

    Traditions:

    Celebrations:

    Foods:

    Vacations or outings:

Why or how did you choose my name?

What is something special about me and/or my family?

Figure 2.1

Korean, Japanese, and Hindu (see Appendix W for more resources). These books became daily read-alouds and led to rich conversations. Mary also sent home a family history survey (see Figure 2.1). When they brought the completed surveys back to class, students identified and marked the various countries of their origins on a large world map. As they discussed all the countries and cultures represented in their classroom, they celebrated their diversity and decided that it's not only okay to be different, it's good to be different!

At the same time, we began to design lessons in the various content areas. Mary's social studies curriculum required her to teach about "needs and wants" and "communities." We knew that we wanted to add a critical perspective to these lessons, but we were unsure how to begin. We spent a lot of time discussing appropriate choices, but we were so focused on *our* ideas about what would be meaningful for the students that we initially overlooked their interests and questions about Hurricane Katrina and the events that were unfolding. When we really listened to them, we were surprised by the intensity of their curiosity about natural disasters. We recognized the opportunity to help them learn to ask critical questions and explore multiple perspectives through current events. This provided a logical connection to the anchor chart of critical questions that Mary wanted students to consider when reading, listening, and interacting (see Figure 1.2).

Adding Perspective to Instruction

Mary follows a predictable routine in the two-and-a-half-hour language arts block she teaches each day, including reading and writing workshop, guided reading with small groups, whole-class instruction and mini-lessons about specific topics of interest or need (such as spelling, grammar, and comprehension strategies), and conferring with students. During this time, students also work in learning centers, and small groups participate in choice activities such as dramatizing stories, illustrating their writing, reading with partners, or working on the computer. A favorite choice activity is interest groups.

In interest groups students meet to explore topics that they want to learn more about. Sometimes the topics emerge from whatever students are curious about at the time, or they may focus on a required unit of study such as space exploration, pioneers, or the environment. When students gain a level of expertise, they share their knowledge with the rest of the class.

The group members may meet informally whenever they can find time or more formally during the language arts block. When the groups begin, students select a topic of interest and may invite classmates to join them. They know they need to fill out an organizer, most often a K-W-L (Ogle 1986) where they record what they "K"now about a topic and then generate a list of content-focused questions: "W"hat they want to know. The "L"—what was learned—represents their work in progress as information is recorded throughout the inquiry.

After starting the K-W-L organizer, students generate a list of resources they will need. During these first stages, Mary helps her students record ideas, identify questions, and gather resources. She usually selects books from the classroom and school library and previews and bookmarks a few safe Internet sources. Her older students learn to do these steps independently and are also able to use safe search engines such as iGoogle, netTrekker, and Yahooligans! to collect Internet-based resources. Mary asks her students to keep a written record of where they obtain informa-

Figure 2.2

CITING SOURCES	
Book	• Author's name • Book title in *italics* • Copyright date Winter, J., *Roberto Clemente: Pride of the Pittsburgh Pirates,* 2005.
Article from Web Resource	• Subject in quotation marks • Author's name (if available) or Web title • Web source or Web address in *italics* • Search engine (if applicable) • Date (if available) or cite "online" "Roberto Clemente," Smithsonian Institution: Beyond Baseball: The Life of Roberto Clemente, *http://www.robertoclemente .si.edu/*netTrekker, online.

tion. First graders record a book title, author, or url address; older students use a simple bibliographic form (see Figure 2.2).

School policy prohibits students from using Wikipedia and Google, and first graders have been allowed to use Internet sources only recently. Mary discusses responsible Internet use with her students. In these brief mini-lessons taught before students begin to use the computers in her classroom, Mary reviews the posted critical questions and encourages the students to refer to them. She also introduces beginning critical media literacy skills, such as requiring students to consider the sources of their information, the copyright dates, and the perspective of the author or designer.

The amount of time students spend researching and investigating varies depending on the topic, level of interest, and availability of resources. Motivation is the catalyst for all ages. When students understand the purpose of their work and have opportunities to make choices and pursue their own questions, they are inspired to participate in interest groups, which quickly become a favorite activity. Because first graders are learning routines, it does take time and practice before they are comfortable with group expectations and collaborative work. But the payoff is that by the time they reach third grade, they need only a quick review of expectations before they are ready to pursue interest groups. Mary uses mini-lessons to reinforce skills such as how to organize materials, share their learning, ask relevant questions, and stay focused on a topic. Figure 2.3 (see also Appendix D) shows the guidelines she uses for interest groups.

INTEREST GROUP START-UP GUIDE	
Getting Started	Select a topic of interest: • Content area (for example: environment, animal habitats) • Subject choice Form a group (usually 4–6 students). Begin an assessment planning document.
Organizing	Use an organizer (for example: K-W-L or semantic map) to: • Record prior knowledge (K). • Record questions—content & critical questions (W). Gather resources: • Print • Digital • Other
Researching	Explore your topic. Take notes or write down important information (L). Add new questions and continue searching. Build a report, written or digital (wiki). Include pictures, photos, music. Record your sources. • Write down the author, title, and/or URL.
Presenting	Create a sharing plan. Use the assessment planning document to consider the following: • Content • Intent • Audience • Composition/design • Social action • Reflection Construct final product (i.e., slideshow, podcast, video). Share!

Figure 2.3

Expanding the Curriculum Through Critical Connections and Authentic Engagements

Using interest groups helped us discover ways to add a critical perspective not only to instruction and assessment in general, but also to the required curriculum across content areas. Our understanding of interest groups

Figure 2.4
Venn Diagram:
Expanding
Curriculum

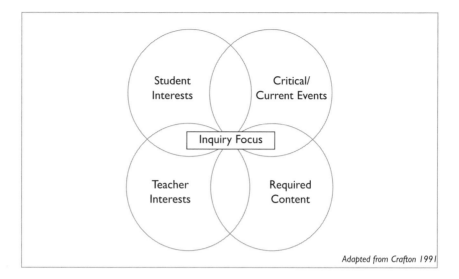

Adapted from Crafton 1991

evolved from a curricular model developed by Crafton (1991) showing the interrelationships between the required curriculum (including standards, outcomes, and benchmarks), the actual enacted curriculum stemming from critical and current events, the students' interests and areas of expertise, and the teacher's areas of interest and expertise. Conceived as a four-way Venn diagram, the model shows that teachers can link critical inquiry to the curriculum by intersecting these components (see Figure 2.4).

For example, Figure 2.5 shows Mary's first-grade curriculum and the various ways it can be expanded to include a critical perspective, along with possibilities for adopting an inquiry stance, exploring multiple perspectives, and engaging in authentic learning experiences.

This expanded model can be adapted to meet the requirements of any curriculum (see Appendix E for a blank template). Some of the critical connections can be planned for unit themes, such as wellness or the environment. Other authentic engagements can occur spontaneously in the classroom or school (such as an incident on the playground). Events such as Hurricane Katrina provide an organic extension of a responsive curriculum that provides a place for student inquiry while still addressing the required units of study. The critical connections in the model represent ways that Mary could follow her students' lead and focus on what interests them. The authentic engagements might incorporate important current events or highlight local or global events, but they are all designed to raise critical questions and help students learn to consider taking social action when and wherever they can.

WAYS TO EXPAND THE CURRICULUM WITH A CRITICAL INQUIRY FOCUS

First-Grade Curriculum	Critical Connections	Authentic Engagements
• Health • Family/relationships	• Wellness focus: news clips featuring nutritional concerns, childhood obesity, environmental health • Stereotypes: gender, elderly issues	• Mrs. Obama's interest in school lunch programs • "Smoke-free" campaign in Illinois • Intergenerational tea
• Needs & wants • Goods & services • Citizenship • Rights & responsibilities	• Consumerism—Whose interests are being served? • Martin Luther King, Jr. • Issues in the news (current events) • Civil rights • Animal rights	• Holiday advertisements and commercials • Grandma Ruth • Hurricane Katrina • Earthquakes in Japan
• Habitats	• Perspectives on zoos • Habitat destruction • "Go green"	• Habitat destruction • "Green" efforts and "make a difference" campaigns

Figure 2.5

🌍 A Responsive Curriculum

"What happened to the animals in the zoos during the hurricane?" Becca wondered one day.

"What about the schools?" Carly wanted to know. "Do they have school right now, and what happened to all their books and supplies during the flood?"

"And what about the people in the Superzone when they needed food for the children and blankets?" Andrew asked, referring to the thousands of displaced people who fled to the Louisiana Superdome.

Blake continued reassuring his classmates, backed by his continual research on the topic. "Well it's still the hurricane season, and there could be more," he said. "They have no protection now because the levees are broken. I'm going to make a book about all the weather disasters so we can learn about them."

Initially all the students were interested in the devastation caused by Hurricane Katrina. It became the topic of many discussions. As the students and Mary gathered books, articles, and Internet resources to inform our conversations, we realized that even as Mary's students were *learning to read* they were simultaneously *reading to learn* by interpreting the images and stories. Mary set up a classroom display of materials related to hurricanes and Katrina, in particular. Asking critical questions such as "Who wrote this article? What do you think the photographer was trying to convey?" helped students consider the people and perspectives behind the news.

As weeks went by, many students selected new activities for their interest groups, but one group of five students sustained an interest in the hurricane and its effect on the people of New Orleans throughout the rest of the school year. The ongoing inquiry from this group of students became a transformational learning piece for everyone!

The Hurricane Interest Group

Right from the start, these five children took control of their learning and immersed themselves in finding out more about hurricanes, particularly about Katrina. They used the class resource chart and all the multimodal tools at their disposal to locate information from various sources. They collected and shared articles and pictures from newspapers, books, and magazines. In class they used safe search sites such as Yahooligans! and Ask Kids to locate information on the Web. At home they watched nightly news reports and asked their parents to help them gather more information for their projects.

The students had a keen awareness of the significance of their work, and they were inspired by learning about something that was happening in real time. They were eager to find materials for each other and share new insights and ideas for teaching the class about their research. In the process of working on individual projects about Hurricane Katrina, they were also working together toward common goals: to understand the devastation of the hurricane, to figure out what happened, and to decide what action they could take to help make a difference.

Blake had a special interest in science, and he was intent on writing a book about weather. It was typical of him to run into class excitedly, waving a folder in the air: "We went on the Internet last night . . . did you know that a hurricane has an eye? Look!" Next he pulled out a diagram and paper filled with text printed from a Web site. Now he had a captive audience. "It's called the eye of the storm. It's not a real eye, but it's a safe place . . ." and he continued to describe his discoveries. Although he couldn't always read the words in the many reports he collected, he had a strong understanding of the content and an ability to read pictures, graphs, and diagrams.

Becca was the group's safety expert. She thought the hurricane victims should have been better prepared with drills—like the fire drills or tornado drills students knew from school. "We can create an information book of safety tips," she said to the group as she and a friend started designing pamphlets.

Raquel used movement and drama to help her understand the impact of the hurricane on its victims. She created a hurricane dance and pranced all around the classroom, inviting others to join in her "dance of destruction." Her lively dramatizations helped the whole group empathize with the victims and brainstorm creative ways they could help.

Andrew, the artist and writer of the group, composed an important informational piece complete with illustrations about how the victims were trapped in the "Superzone" (see Figure 2.6).

Carly, the self-proclaimed leader of the group and the driving force in helping the group stay focused on the social issues, ultimately persuaded the whole class to become active in the cause.

As the Hurricane Group members (shown in Figure 2.7) researched, worked, and talked together about their learning, they developed a very strong bond. They began to sit together in the lunchroom and play

Figure 2.6
Andrew's Informational Drawing of Hurricane Katrina Victims in the Superdome
("Some people had money and could buy things and get out when the hurricane happened but the poor people were poor and couldn't buy things and couldn't survive and went to the Superzone [Superdome] to be safe but they weren't.")

Figure 2.7
Members of the
Hurricane Group

together at recess, and long after other interest groups had moved on to other topics, they continued to bring in materials that would help each other learn more about their own special inquiry.

Critical Connections

The Hurricane Group members continued their explorations and became very well informed about weather disasters. But we began to wonder if they understood how the devastation and aftermath had particularly imperiled and disenfranchised the poorest residents of New Orleans. Penny had lived in New Orleans and was eager to raise some critical issues that would help Mary's young students understand that the people most adversely affected by Hurricane Katrina were poor, black residents who lived in the part of the city that was most vulnerable to flooding. We both wanted to delve into the injustices of this situation and use this incident for critical inquiry. However, always mindful of the need to make sure a topic was appropriate for her students, Mary wondered if her students were ready for an exploration of race and poverty. We decided to talk with the Hurricane Group and carefully guide a conversation that focused on who the victims were, why so many were left behind, and what more could have been done to help them.

Penny: So—who are the people who are the victims of the hurricane? Why do you think some got out and others couldn't?

Carly: The poor people stayed behind because they didn't have cars or couldn't afford the gas.

Penny: Who were these poor people?

Becca (ignoring Penny's question): I bet they were hot inside with no air conditioning.

Penny: What could have been done for them? Their houses were all gone or flooded. I have good friends who live in New Orleans. They had to pack up whatever would fit into their car and drive out of the city to a safe place away from the hurricane. They could get out. But some people couldn't and, actually, some people wouldn't.

Take a look at this picture on the cover of the magazine [*Newsweek*, Sept. 12, 2005]. What do you notice? What's going on here?

Carly: It's a mother with two children—she's carrying two babies and running from the flooding. I think she needs milk to feed them.

Raquel: She looks really scared.

Becca: Look, see the water in the street, and she's running with the kids. Why didn't she just drive out of town like your friends before the hurricane came?

Penny: Good question. She sure didn't get out. Why do you think that happened? Do you notice anything about her?

Carly: Yeah, she's mad or scared, and probably wondering how she's going to take care of the babies—with no diapers, no milk, not even water to drink.

Mary: You are really doing a great job of reading the pictures. What words would you use as you read the pictures? What words would describe this picture? Can you write them down around the picture? These words will tell a story, too.

On a piece of paper the children wrote these words: *mad, worried, scared, hungry, tired, fainting, disastrously, devastated,* and *hell* (qualified by saying "not a *bad* word"), and *help.* Then they decided to write what they thought would be "safe things" or things that the woman could use to be safe: *blankets, water, food, clothes,* and *a way to get out.*

Penny (looking closely at the picture with the children): Do you know that many of the people who couldn't get out of New Orleans were poor and African American?

Mary: How do you feel about the people who couldn't get out? Do you think that's fair? Do you think that others should have been helping

more? We've been talking about being good citizens. Citizens have
rights and responsibilities. Do we, as citizens, have the right to be
helped when we are in need? Do we have the responsibility to help
others? What could people do to help? Do you think we should do
something?

Raquel: On Nickelodeon [a television network] they are doing a
backpack project. I'd like to do a project.

Carly: Let's look up the hurricane information online. There may be
some ideas about what we can do to help.

Blake: And I can find more pictures. We can print them and add them to
our book.

Mary: Great ideas. Before you work on your projects, I'd like to take one
more look at this picture. I think it is important that we try to
understand how hard it was for the people in New Orleans, especially
those who were left behind. Let's see if we can act out what is going
on here. Based on what you know about New Orleans and the
hurricane, what characters would be in our drama story? Who wants
to be the mother [Carly]; the young child [Raquel]; the baby [Becca];
the rescue worker [Andrew]; the store owner [Blake]?

One of Mary's favorite instructional strategies is dramatizing a story.
This kind of process drama helps students put themselves "in someone
else's shoes," making it easier for them to understand others' perspectives.
The children love acting, too, and easily assumed their roles as they interpreted running for safety to the Louisiana Superdome as the flood waters
rushed into the city. The entire class watched the performance and was
immediately interested, leading to a passionate discussion about the victims of Katrina, led by the Hurricane Group.

Carly started the class discussion by asking: "Did you know that most
of the people who couldn't get out of the flood were African Americans?"
Most of the children were astonished. "We read this picture on the cover of
a magazine," added Becca, "and it was a mother who couldn't get milk for
her babies. She was upset and scared, and it's not right. She needed help
and everyone left her behind—and all the people in the Superdome, too."

🌍 Scaffolding Student Understanding

It was fascinating to listen to the children share their insights. Just minutes
ago, they didn't see the racial discrimination or injustices in this incident.

Now they could name the injustices, but they still didn't really understand them.

A focus on African-American history was closely connected to the first-grade social studies curriculum that included rights, responsibilities, citizenship, and biographies of famous people, including Dr. Martin Luther King. These topics were also aligned with the language arts reading and writing goals and standards, so Mary felt comfortable adding a social justice component. The connections provided a smooth transition to a critical extension of the curriculum, in which Mary was able to include African-American culture and history through interactive read-alouds and class discussions. This helped build background knowledge so that the children could have a deeper understanding of the primary victims of Hurricane Katrina.

Mary's class had no African-American students this particular year, so we thought it was particularly important for the children to understand the heritage of African Americans and to do so in the context of the students' own cultures. One of the first books Mary read aloud was an excerpt from *Mr. Bojangles* (Haskins 1999), a selection from her basal reading series. This book tells the true story of a famous African-American tap dancer and celebrates his contributions to music. It is a lively tale that had students joining in the chorus and tap dancing around the room. The phrase, "he made music with his feet," opened up conversations that supported multiliteracies and the many ways that communication includes words, gestures, music, movement, and pictures. Akshita made connections when she shared how important dance is to her Indian culture and brought in photographs of her own dance celebrations. The students were excited and brought the book to music class to perform for the music teacher.

Mary next introduced jazz and blues music, which some children knew about because of the famous House of Blues in Chicago (Figure 2.8). As the class listened to the music and discussed the words embedded in the songs, they began to learn about the difficulties as well as the accomplishments of African Americans in history. The soulful blues and tantalizing jazz melodies helped the children better understand issues at an emotional as well as an intellectual level.

We compiled a text set of materials that included books and read-alouds to extend their interest and background knowledge. We brought in books from the school and public libraries, found relevant Web sites and magazines, and posted enlarged pictures from Faith Ringgold's beautiful books and tapestries about famous African Americans. One of the children's favorite read-alouds was *Amazing Grace* (Hoffman 1991), the story

Figure 2.8
Raquel's Rendition
of Jazz and Blues

of a young African-American girl who wants to be Peter Pan in a school play and faces challenges concerning both gender and race.

"Natalie didn't want Grace to be Peter Pan in *Amazing Grace*," Megan stated emphatically.

"Right," Carly added, "because she was black and a girl."

Because the boys were very quiet, Mary asked her standard inquiry question, "So what do you think about that?"

"It wasn't fair," Andrew said. "Grace could be anything she wanted to be. Nobody thought she could do it, but her grandmother gave her courage and she tried out for the part and made it, even though she was a girl."

Gender was the dominant issue for the children. It took much more time and more scaffolding for them to notice race as a social issue (see Figure 2.9). *Ben's Trumpet* (1991) by Rachel Isadora was another selection that Mary read to the class. This wonderful picture book describes a young boy's fascination with the saxophone and the Zig Zag jazz club. It also explores poverty and caring for others, as Ben plays his imaginary horn. Through Mary's guided discussion of this book, students began to recognize and understand the poverty in the story and explore how Ben's lifestyle was so different from their own. Other books that Mary read as part of this thematic text set included *White Socks Only* (Coleman 1996),

Figure 2.9
Ruby Bridges's
Daily Walk to
Integrate Frantz
Elementary School

The Other Side (Woodson 2001), and *Sister Anne's Hands* (Lorbiecki 1998). Listening carefully to her students' discussions, she continued searching for ways to help them connect these new insights with their own personal histories and interests.

Story painting was another favorite activity that Mary often used to extend and interpret class read-alouds. Sometimes she asked the "story painters" to write captions for their pictures, representing a significant idea from the story through both print and images (see Figure 2.10). Students also practiced retelling and reading stories fluently and with expression, through reader's theater, dance, drama, drawings, and music.

Mary continued scaffolding her students' understanding of poverty and discrimination with picture books appropriate for first grade. She designed opportunities for her students to understand and express their insights in multimodal ways, using music, dance, drama, and art. As the lead learner in the classroom, Mary was acutely aware of her influence over her students' thinking and actions. She paid careful attention to her own words and actions and worked hard to honor different points of view.

Critical Word Wall

Close to Dr. Martin Luther King's birthday in January, Mary selected the book *Martin's Big Words* (Rappaport 2001) as a read-aloud. This book pro-

Figure 2.10

STORY PAINTING EXTENSIONS

This is a favorite activity that supports class read-alouds. It is most often used with chapter books. After listening to and discussing a chapter, two students are selected to be story painters and summarizers. Their task is to summarize the reading, capturing the main ideas of the chapter, in both words and images using watercolors or their choice of painting technique. These creations are shared at the beginning of the next read-aloud session. When the book is finished, all paintings are compiled and made into a big book for the classroom library.

Questions that support this activity include:

- What colors will capture the mood of the chapter?
- How will you depict the characters?
  - Where will they be placed on the paper?
  - How will you use size and perspective?
- What do you want the viewer to notice first or most?
- How can you share the main ideas in the chapter?
- How will you support these big ideas?

An interesting result of this activity is that the summary becomes easy for students to write after creating their pictures.

---

vided significant insight for the children to understand some of the hardships African Americans endured throughout history. Before reading the book, Mary shared some thoughts with her first graders. She explained how Dr. King was sometimes called a peaceful warrior because he used his words instead of weapons to sting. The children talked about the connotations of that and concluded that words must be very powerful. They brainstormed a list of strong words within this new context, including *courage, love,* and *hope* (see Figure 2.11).

When Mary read the story aloud, each time she said one of the children's identified words, they would gasp and say, "That's one of our words!" Dr. King's words, "When someone says hate, we say love," became the class mantra for the rest of the year. A sign with this mantra, created by Ricky and DJ (Figure 2.12), was displayed on the classroom wall and outside the door. When children disagreed, argued, or got into trouble, their conflict resolution always included these words, which had a calming effect and reminded them of their shared learning experience about Dr. King.

This list led us to start a critical word wall that ultimately contained all the terms we thought were powerful and important to our understanding of the lives of African Americans and other people. It was important for the children to understand that words could portray people in either positive

Figure 2.11 List of BIG Words Created by Tals and Aliyah

Dear Dr.king thank you for all of the thing
you helped us with we apprsheatted with
freedom know king or queen to boss us around.

when
someone say's
hate you say
LoVE. *some bigword's*

Figure 2.12 Class Mantra, Inspired by *Martin's Big Words*

or negative ways and could be interpreted differently depending on someone's experience or background. As the students used the words, dramatized them, illustrated them, and connected them to their personal histories, the new vocabulary became truly interactive (see Figure 2.13).

At this point, we felt safe challenging students to expand their thinking in critical ways, so we introduced a redesigned version of the traditional "Five Ws and an H" question, using it to raise social awareness (see Figure 2.14 and Appendix F). After reading *A Picture Book of Rosa Parks* (Adler 1993) one day, a small group's discussion provided a nice connection.

Figure 2.13

CRITICAL WORD WALL

Our BIG words (in no special order):

- Freedom
- Democracy
- Peace
- Decisions
- Friendship
- Kindness
- Rights
- Bravery
- Care

- Love
- Opportunities
- Togetherness
- Hope
- Understanding
- Responsibilities
- Wisdom
- Powerful
- Life

- Happiness
- Forgiveness
- Faith
- Quest
- Empathy
- Justice
- Free

Figure 2.14

REDESIGNED W-H QUESTIONS

WHO?

- Whose voice is heard? Whose voice is not heard?
- Who is the author (designer/illustrator), and who else could author this piece?
- Who is the audience for this selection, and who else might be interested?

WHAT?

- What perspective is presented? What is another perspective to explore?
- What does the author/illustrator/designer want you to think?
- What are other ways to think about the same idea (topic, event, situation)?

WHERE?

- Where can spaces be opened in the selection for other points of view, ideas, or issues?
- Where did this idea originate, and how could it be more democratic or just?
- Where do authors get ideas?

WHEN?

- When did you notice your thinking changed about the selection?
- When did you engage with this story/design/performance?
- When did you think you understood the selection?

WHY?

- Why did the author choose this genre or these modes for the selection?
- Why do you think this design was selected and for what purpose?
- Why do you think these tools and techniques were used, and what are alternatives?

HOW?

- How can you use this experience to make a difference?
- How do your life experiences affect your understanding and appreciation of the selection?
- How can you use this experience to expand your thinking and to act on your beliefs?

"She was very brave," said Ricardo.

"Yes, like Dr. King and Ruby Bridges," responded Christine.

"She wouldn't give up her seat on the bus. That took courage," replied Jedi.

"She did the right thing," Christine continued. "She had the right to do anything that she wanted to do." Then she added, "Well, I don't know . . . we have rights and responsibilities, but that doesn't mean we can do whatever we want . . . we might hurt someone, it might be dangerous . . ."

"Yes," Blake piped in, "that's why we have laws."

And someone else added, "And responsibilities."

"I like the way this group is thinking," Penny said. "Let's take a look at our redesigned W-H questions. I think you are exploring them as you talk about Rosa. Let's look at the 'who' category."

They studied the list and looked pensive.

"I think Rosa Parks's voice is heard," Christine said. "Well, maybe not her words exactly."

"It's what she *did*," said Jedi, picking up on the insight. "You know, her actions."

"I'm noticing that you are exploring perspective when you recognize that Rosa had rights, but there are limits to rights," Penny said, helping them think about and use words that express critical literacy vocabulary. "Like Christine said, you can't just do anything that you wish. It is such an important statement."

"I sort of did the 'when' question when I stopped to think about rights," Christine said. "I know that you can't just do anything, you know, like break a law. That's when I changed my thinking."

Penny continued, "Good, Christine. I'm wondering if anyone can answer a 'how' question. How does Rosa Parks's story affect you?"

"Well, we know she was brave, and did what she felt was right," Jedi began.

"Yes, and that's hard," Penny responded. "It takes a lot of courage."

Jedi continued, "I think we can learn from her."

"I agree, Jedi. We can learn a lot from her example," Penny confirmed.

Learning Wall

Through our research, we came across the idea of a learning wall or visual audit trail (Vasquez 2003) and were intrigued with the idea of making the students' learning visible and public as a demonstration and documentation of their accomplishments. We recognized the power in visual images, repeated reading of stories, and extended time for discussion and talking together. Using the long bulletin board in the hall outside Mary's classroom, we posted pictures, stories, articles, time lines, biographies, graphs, book reviews, and many other artifacts of the students' studies. This learning wall eventually reflected all their inquiry projects and became a visual portrayal of the social issues her class explored throughout the year. The board became an ongoing, interactive project, and children kept organizing and rearranging the material on the wall to represent their learning and new insights.

Resist was a word that Mary presented to the children during her mini-lessons about interpreting vocabulary from a critical perspective. It's not that she wanted them to become radical activists. She wanted to help them learn that almost everything they read, view, or access on a computer has a particular purpose, intentionally designed by an author (writer, artist, or designer) to influence or connect with a reader's perception of the message. To activate the students' background knowledge and help them understand how they were influenced by texts, images, or Web sites, we brought in newspaper advertisements filled with holiday merchandise. We also looked at pop-up ads on Web sites and ads in magazines. Mary asked the children what they noticed about the layout of the sale ads. Right away, Jessie saw the colors red and black, seemingly jumping off the page. Charlie noticed that children of various ethnicities and ages seemed to be having a lot of fun with the merchandise. Katy identified pictures of popular toys much in demand. Jack noticed lots of numbers and percentages off the original prices.

Mary's students learned that you can attract and influence a potential audience by the design of a paper, advertisement, story, image, or online feature. Similarly, the use of color, placement on a page, font, and pictures used with print can compel a reader or viewer to want to own something. The next step was to help the children learn to "resist" or deconstruct and refuse to accept the intended message, interpret it differently, or reject it altogether. Of course, they always had the right to accept the message—but we wanted them to know it needed to be their conscious choice.

The word *resist* became a symbol of Mary's students' growing awareness of the power of language, the ways they could influence others with their words and pictures, their enhanced ability to infer meaning, and their growing sense of confidence in recognizing and interpreting hidden messages. Along with saying the word, the children also liked to put out their hand, in a "stop" gesture, implying that they were rejecting the intent to buy or want or like something. The physical movement of extending their hands reinforced the importance of the word *resist* coming out of their mouths, making this a powerful learning experience.

"Let's put our big word *resist* in the middle of the bulletin board," said Jackie. "We want everyone to know that we can accept or reject something we see or read."

Andy agreed, "Yep, we don't have to believe everything we hear. Sometimes it's not true, or they even try to *make* us think a certain way about something that we don't like."

Penny overheard the conversation and asked, "What do you mean?"

"Well, remember when we looked at the newspaper ads for toys?" Jenny explained. "We noticed that the big letters in black and red said *sale*, and there were pictures of kids having fun riding the bikes and playing with the dolls. They were trying to get us to buy them even if we didn't need them."

Andrew added, "Yeah, when my dad took us to the car show and pointed out the car he wanted, I told him to resist—he didn't really need a new car! My mom laughed her head off."

A close examination of their work showed the students were using many different multimodal tools including print, color, design, illustrations, and technology. One of their favorite projects on this wall was a time line of African-American history, complete with cutout characters and word bubbles explaining who the characters were and why it was important to know about them.

For any willing visitor, the children loved to go out in the hallway and demonstrate the "Hot Seat" strategy (see Figure 2.15). One day they were showing Penny their time line in the hall when the principal walked by. She was transfixed as she saw students standing in front of the bulletin board next to identified historic African Americans. Acting in the role of characters on the wall, the children were able to answer questions asked by others, showing that they clearly understood their character's personality and the importance of the historic events being portrayed.

"Why did you refuse to give up your seat on the bus?" Jenny asked Teri, who was portraying Rosa Parks.

"Because I have a right to sit anywhere on the bus just like a white person," Teri answered. "We are all human beings, and we should all be treated fairly."

Deciding to jump in, the principal then turned to Susie who was portraying Ruby Bridges and asked, "Weren't you scared going into that school while everyone was shouting at you?"

Figure 2.15

HOT SEAT STRATEGY

Students assume the identities of historical figures or characters in a book. Classmates ask questions of the characters, and the student who receives a question answers in character. For example, a student assumes the role of Dr. King, and a classmate asks, "Dr. King, why did you organize a bus boycott?" and Dr. King might answer, "I felt that we African Americans needed to support Rosa Parks, and we needed to do this in a nonviolent way . . ." Hot Seat is an open-ended activity designed to support character analysis and comprehension.

Susie answered in character, "Yes, but I was praying and that helped me get into the school safely. And you know what? I learned a lot being the only child in school that year. The teacher would have had nothing to do if I wasn't there."

Jumping in, Drew asked Timmy, who was representing Martin Luther King, "Why didn't you want to fight the people who were attacking you?"

Timmy replied, "Because fighting doesn't make anything better. You can make a bigger difference by being nice and trying to love each other. Remember [and the whole class chimed in], 'when someone says hate, we say love!'"

Asking critical questions, exploring perspectives, using process drama, and engaging in rich discussions about historical figures helped the students internalize the issues and injustices they were discussing. They also gained a clearer understanding of how they, as responsible citizens, could do something to make a difference. In turn, this recognition also helped the students make critical connections to better understand the poverty and circumstances of many of the Hurricane Katrina victims. Armed with greater knowledge and understanding, the students revealed an emerging desire to help the victims in some way.

Taking Responsible Action

The Hurricane Group remained a tightly knit group throughout the year, continuing to research weather phenomena and hurricanes. They naturally gravitated toward each other and met to share information whenever there was a break in the day or they were offered choice-time opportunities. But it wasn't until the group members shared their artifacts and research with the entire class that we saw how much these five children had evolved in their thinking and how they had progressed in their transformation into socially responsible individuals. With the help of the school technology teacher, the children put together a slideshow of their learning about Katrina, and their enthusiasm spilled over into the whole classroom, challenging the rest of the students to join them in finding a way to help the hurricane victims.

With Mary's guidance, each member of the Hurricane Group organized new interest groups within the class. They divided up the work to find out more about hurricanes, families affected by the hurricane, environmental issues related to flooding, how animals were affected (pets and zoo animals), and what happened to the schools. As all the children in the class read (books, encyclopedias, newspapers, magazines), viewed (pictures, Web sites, Internet sources), listened (podcasts, music), discussed, and dramatized situations (improvisation, reader's theater), we could see evidence that they were using the language of critical literacy and looking for ways to make a difference (see Figure 2.16).

Figure 2.16

HURRICANE KATRINA INTEREST GROUPS: WHAT CAN WE DO TO HELP?

Interest Group	Questions	Key Ideas	Possible Actions

Families	• Are the basic needs of families being met?
	  - Food
	  - Water
	  - Shelter
	  - Love & care
		Families have lost their homes. Some family members have been lost, have died, or have been separated from each other. People are sending care packages and helping.	American Red Cross is sending first-aid and care packages. People are giving victims a place to live.

Environment & Animals	• What has happened to the habitats?
	  - Can the animals survive?
	  - Can they meet their basic needs?
	  - What about people's pets?
	  - Have they found new homes?
	  - Have they been reunited with their owners?
		Pets are being rescued. Many pets survived, but they need homes. People are looking for their pets.	American Humane Society is helping with rescues. Petfinder.com will help people look for their pets.

Schools	• Are children back in their schools?
	  - Do they have the supplies they need?
	  - Books? Do they have enough?
		There are schools that need to be rebuilt. Some schools lost all their books. Students need supplies.	Nickelodeon is collecting backpacks and supplies. We can share our supplies and books.*

Hurricanes	• What causes hurricanes?
	  - How can we plan to be safe when it's hurricane season?
	  - What can we learn from this disaster?
		Hurricanes are tropical storms that happen over oceans. They have high winds that cause lots of damage (like a tornado). Listen for watches and warnings.	Have a hurricane safety plan:
			• emergency supplies
			• evacuation plan
			
			*Our Action Plan!

Hurricane Katrina provided opportunities for the children to learn about the rights and responsibilities of citizenship. With carefully scaffolded conversations, they were able to empathize and recognize the poverty and injustice that accompanied Hurricane Katrina, and they were moved to take action.

Carly: We started out being sad, and now we're mad.

Mary: What do you mean?

Carly: Well, we were sad because people lost their homes and couldn't go to school. The poor people were left behind, and they were not helped by the rich people who left and they weren't helped enough by the government.

Blake: Yeah, it wasn't fair.

Mary: What do you mean?

Blake: It wasn't fair that a lot of the black people couldn't leave because they had no money.

Raquel: I wonder if they played jazz and blues in the Superdome because that music showed their feelings and made them feel better.

Andrew: They had to learn to resist and be powerful so they could get out if it happened again.

Penny: Resist what?

Andrew: Resist living in a house that could fall apart in a storm; resist people telling them they can't leave; or find a way to get out before the storm—to ask for help.

Becca: Yeah, like when Ruby Bridges went into the school even though the white kids didn't want her to. She didn't let them tell her she couldn't go.

Mary: Why don't you all turn and talk to a partner and discuss what that must have been like.

Mary (afterward): So, what did you all talk about?

Carly: We were thinking that since there were no other kids, Ruby could have her choice of reading any book in the school. But then we wondered if the books in some schools got ruined in the hurricane.

Penny: Actually, as you know, when I lived in New Orleans, I was a teacher in the same school Ruby Bridges attended, and I know that school flooded badly. So what do you think we could do to show we care and to help? I heard that a lot of schools have no books—or very few.

Carly: We could bring in some of our own or have a book sale to raise money.

Blake: I could bring some of my books from home to send to them.

Raquel: Maybe we could sell cookies.

Andrew: Well—I have books to bring in, too, but I have to ask my mom.

Mary: That's a great plan. Let's write letters to our parents to tell them that we want to send books to a school in New Orleans since their books were lost in the hurricane.

Carly: But no torn books or dog-chewed books. These have to be nice.

Mary: Okay, gently used books—in good condition—letter to the parents—anything else?

Carly: Yes, we need to find a school we can send them to—I'll look online for one.

Penny: I'll work on that with you, too.

Becca: I'll write an e-mail to the school custodian for some boxes.

Carly: And I'll organize the class to pack up the books and tape the boxes.

Andrew: I'll make a poster for the hall.

Raquel: And maybe the student council could announce it to the whole school.

Mary: That's a great idea. Good for you! It could be something that other classes might like to take on. Definitely talk about it at the student council meeting. So you think we, as citizens, have a responsibility to help others? What are we learning here?

Carly: Well, we learned about the victims of the hurricane as well as what a hurricane is. We also learned that it was mostly poor and black people who couldn't get out, and we can do something to help.

Mary and the children wrote letters to their parents explaining what they planned to do and why (Figure 2.17), and when the books started to come in, Carly and the original Hurricane Group organized the collection and got the rest of the class to help pack the books in cartons (Figure 2.18).

Figure 2.17
Kevin's Letter to
His Parents

Dear Mom and Dad,

Plez send in books to help kids
in New Orlens. Its OK if there
uzed but good. We care!

Love,
Kevin

An Internet search helped us track down a first-grade classroom in New Orleans that desperately needed books to replace those lost in the flooding. The students addressed the boxes and included a class picture and words of encouragement to the recipients, and Mary sent the boxes off to New Orleans.

Through this powerful critical inquiry experience, the Hurricane Group members and their classmates demonstrated their responsibilities as citizens and learned that caring involves action to help make a differ-

Figure 2.18
Sending Books to
Victims of
Hurricane Katrina

ence. At the end of first grade, Mary's students were able to articulate this
critical dimension of care:

Mary: This whole year, we've been talking about caring for each other.
We've been saying, "When someone says hate, we say love," from our
book about Dr. Martin Luther King. So, what does it mean to care?

Gaby: Well, you have to do it, you can't just say, "I care." You have to
actually do it!

Mary: Okay, so what does that look like? Jason, can you think of any
examples or what were you going to say?

Jason: I was going to say the same as Gaby.

Mary: Yes, Sonya—go ahead.

Sonya: Like what Gaby said, I know a connection. You have to be—you
help a person. That's a community who cares, like not leaving them
alone or like bringing them to the nurse. Like my dad, he fell down. I
took care of him.

Mary: Awesome. Gaby, what did you want to add?

Gaby: A connection with what Sonya said, if you're playing like at the
park and someone is sitting there on a bench, you can ask them to
play and like be their friend.

Mary: Very good—you boys and girls are talking about how we care
about our family and we care about our friends. We care about our
school. [Alex's hand goes up.] What other things do we care about?

Alex: Here's what I think. We shouldn't just care for people, but for the
environment, and some people don't exactly care for the

environment. So it's up to us as children and citizens and a community who cares to care for it.

Mary: I would agree with that.

Alex: Some people actually do the opposite of caring for it, so it's up to us to care for it.

Mary: Yes, you are going to be the adults who will take care of the planet and you have a big responsibility . . .

Alex: Yes, but first we have to start it out as children right now.

The students cared deeply about each other, and we realized that they could understand principles such as fairness and justice and apply them to global issues (Noddings 1992). A classroom culture of care helped us negotiate tough issues that some educators might question as inappropriate for first graders. But we felt an obligation to openly and honestly address questions and concerns about issues that young students are exposed to (including war, natural disasters, homelessness, and crime). A focus on care in support of a critical perspective expanded the students' thinking and learning about living in harmony with nature, about rights and responsibilities, and about citizenship and what it means to live in a democracy. We also addressed the curricular expectations in ways that resonated authentically with the children and helped them learn lessons that surpassed district expectations.

We gained confidence in addressing important social issues with young learners and discovered that critical literacy can become a way of life—in the classroom and beyond. We learned to live our beliefs, to trust that students in a classroom community of practice can learn the prescribed curriculum and much more, and that authentic learning experiences with a focus on critical social action can be transformational for everyone.

In May of 2011 we witnessed the impact of our critical literacy work when Ricardo missed school to participate in the immigration rallies that were held in downtown Chicago. He told the class he was marching in the rally with his family, and we were all concerned about his safety and the possibility of demonstrators becoming involved in fights with the police. But when he returned to school, he told us how he had marched "peacefully, just like Dr. King" with his mother, father, siblings, cousins, and grandparents, carrying a sign that said, "Whatever happened to justice for all?" The children immediately connected with the word *justice* from the critical word wall and celebrated Ricardo's bravery and courage.

TEACHER TALK *Insights & Emerging Understandings*

When a classroom becomes a community of practice, all the members work toward both individual goals and shared experiences agreed upon by the group. This provides many and varied opportunities for individual inquiries that ultimately enrich the entire community. Interest groups can provide opportunities for students to engage in focused inquiries about issues and ideas that matter to them while still learning the content, skills, and strategies identified in the required curriculum. During these group experiences, students learn to work collaboratively and to care about each other. Care takes on a deeper meaning and obligation as students assume responsibility for events in their daily lives and develop a global perspective as they learn about the world beyond the classroom.

The social aspect of learning, embodied in communities of practice, is one of the foundations of critical literacy, and an important component of all learning. When children are provided with materials, tools, strategies, background information, and a compelling purpose to learn, even the youngest learners can engage in critical inquiry and take action to make a difference.

Curriculum and instruction naturally expand to include critical connections and authentic engagements across the curriculum and in all subject areas. Sometimes, as shown in the Hurricane Katrina example, big issues or events support critical engagements. Other times it is the incidental everyday, authentic classroom experiences that provide opportunities for students to consider different points of view, explore alternative perspectives, learn to respect each other's contributions, and work toward shared understandings.

Getting Started

() Start by establishing a critical community of practice focusing on community building and social action.

- Establish classroom routines and a structure that allows for independent group work focused on student interests. These interests can pertain to particular units of study, current events, or students' special areas of expertise.

- Make "caring" a core component of the classroom community by helping students understand that *care* is a both a noun and a verb and that it implies demonstration in some meaningful way (toward each other, within the classroom and school, and in the community).

- Look for real experiences and critical connections that provide powerful motivation for genuine engagement in everyday, local, and global events. Help students become aware of issues and ways they can make a difference.

() Design opportunities for critical inquiry and scaffold and address authentic issues.

- Use critical read-alouds and text sets (see Appendixes R–X).
- Form interest groups.
- Model and post redesigned W-H questions.
- Build a critical word wall.
- Create a learning wall (audit trail) to capture student inquiry and critical work.

Remember that young children can engage in critical inquiries. Our job is to scaffold and support their learning in developmentally appropriate ways. A critical community of practice provides a safe environment for addressing tough issues, even for young children. Caring implies that we need to help young children understand that they can use their learning to make a difference through responsible action.

Favorite Multicultural Books with Critical Potential
(See Appendix W for more text suggestions.)
Amazing Grace by M. Hoffman
Angel Child, Dragon Child by M. Seurat
The Butter Battle Book by Dr. Seuss
Chrysanthemum by K. Henkes
The Color of Home by M. Hoffman
I Hate English! by E. Levine
My Name Is Yoon by H. Recorvits
The Other Side by J. Woodson
Sister Anne's Hands by M. Lorbiecki
Smoky Night by E. Bunting
The Story of Ruby Bridges by R. Coles
Tar Beach by F. Ringgold
White Socks Only by E. Coleman
White Wash by N. Shange

Chapter 3

Go Green!
The Language of
Multiliteracies

"Here's a reminder about the PTO's special lunch day next Thursday," Mary announces, handing out a bright green flyer to her students.

"Not another one," Tyler groans. "We've already had three notes."

Naomi, using her most serious voice, rolls her eyes and comments, "They're wasting so much paper!"

Another round of concerned student voices picks up her thread: "They're destroying trees." "They're hurting the environment." "They need to 'go green!'"

Then Collette reminds everyone that her mom is in charge of the PTO special lunch. Logan senses an opportunity and suggests sending Collette's mom an e-mail message asking the Parent Teacher Organization to "go green," eliminate the paper reminders, and use the computer to send messages "from now on!"

By this point in the school year Mary's students are well aware that literacy involves more than reading and writing print materials or using oral language. They have been using many forms of expression such as singing, dancing, drawing, painting, writing, and acting, and learning to use a variety of multimodal tools (especially technology) to learn about and change the world.

🌍 Environmental Activists

Most primary grades have units about the environment. In Mary's classroom, students participate in interest groups that explore endangered animals, global warming, and the need to reduce, reuse, and recycle. A lot of teacher planning goes into preparing for these studies: gathering related fiction and nonfiction materials for guided reading groups, selecting appropriate Web sites for interest group inquiries, and filling baskets with related books, magazines, and articles, as well as paper, crayons, and markers for student investigations and research. Mary also meets with the resource teachers (English language learners, technology, special education, and reading specialist) to plan appropriate interventions for some of her students.

Interest groups are part of Mary's morning literacy block. During that time, her students apply what they are learning in other areas of the required curriculum. There is a predictable structure for working together as they practice the literacy skills and strategies she has been teaching throughout the year. The students know the rules and expectations that help the classroom run smoothly. Students understand that they are resources for each other and know who to go to for questions or problems if Mary is busy. For example, on the front bulletin board, there is a large "Technology Helpers" chart where students' names are posted with their areas of digital expertise (see Figure 3.1). These class helpers include students like Allen, an expert on downloading photographs, or Victor, a wiz at spelling and editing, or Nidhi, who can add music and digital effects to their slideshows. Everyone knows to consult that chart before going to the teacher to get help. In addition, baskets of sticky notes are always available during work time. If students need Mary's help

Figure 3.1

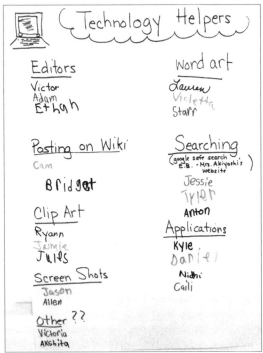

while she is busy with a group or in a conference, they are encouraged to post a note on the door for her response when she is available. They also know they can browse the notes and reply to each other.

To ensure that no time is wasted looking for supplies and materials during interest group time, all students have personal folders that include organizers, checklists, and notes, as well as computer document folders. They may also have favorite bookmarked sites from kid-friendly search engines or an approved list prepared by the computer lab teacher and Mary. Students are responsible for keeping materials organized, and they may add resources to the supply of books, magazines, and reference materials that Mary has assembled for each topic. Classroom computers are assigned using a rotation system, and if a computer becomes available, anyone can use it as needed.

Mary acquired iPads through a district grant, and her students immediately set up a checklist so everyone would get a turn to use them. Most students now prefer to use the iPads for their inquiry investigations, and they have become very protective of the devices, making sure they are charged and stored properly. We are continually amazed by their intuitive expertise using these computers without instruction, other than the usual rules for sharing and cautions about Internet safety. For example, one morning, Mary was startled by an alarm and a message that appeared on the screen of one of the iPads. Wondering what was going on, she saw these words slowly emerging on the screen: *"Check to see if the iPad is charged, make sure your hands are clean, and use responsibly."* A little sleuthing led to Caili, who confidently told Mary, "Oh, I put an alarm on the iPads as a reminder to follow the rules for using them and taking good care of them."

Interest groups are part of the daily routine, and weekly and daily schedules posted in the room help Mary's students function independently within the classroom parameters. They know when they are meeting with Mary in guided groups, and students who are working independently know that some well-loved learning centers are always available (e.g., reader's theater, library center, and story painting). There may also be content-area centers, which change with the subject, unit, or student inquiries. All students understand that they are required to visit specific centers for skill and strategy practice. But when time and scheduling permit, the students most often choose to work on their interest group projects. The students know they can meet informally as a group in different areas of the room to talk and work together.

There is such a high level of engagement in Mary's classroom that when Penny or any visitor walks in, nobody notices. On any given morning, Mary usually meets with a guided reading group around a table in the center of the room. On this particular day, she is helping her students read nonfiction books about the environment. The ELL teacher is working with a group of children on their research about recycling and why it is important. A parent/grandparent volunteer is listening to several children practicing a reader's theater presentation. Other children are story painting and writing captions for their illustrations of *The Great Kapok Tree* (Cherry 1990). A small group is writing a new version of *The Lorax* (Seuss 1971) before posting it on the class Web page. Another group is creating a plan for the school to recycle lunch trays and reduce the amount of garbage and waste, emphasizing what the children call "the three Rs" (reduce, reuse, and recycle).

Glancing around the room, we see students applying conventional print skills and strategies while becoming increasingly sophisticated and confident in their use of technology. Several students are using computers, creating slideshows, or writing and illustrating their inquiry (research) reports. Three other children are recording the results of a class survey about favorite lunches on a spreadsheet, using Mary's own laptop (Figure 3.2). As they become more confident using visual and digital communication skills during the literacy block, they are able to transfer the skills to other subjects. And with an emphasis on critical literacy, the students are also realizing that they can use print, visual, and digital tools to make their voices heard or take action that will make a difference for themselves and for others.

Figure 3.2
Collaborative
Computer Work

🌏 "Let's Read the Pictures"

Walking around the classroom, Penny joins Paul and Lainie, who are reading *The World That Jack Built* (Brown 1991), a picture book about pollution based on the rhyme, "The House That Jack Built."

Paul: Dr. Silvers, this is a great book!

Penny: Tell me about it.

Paul: It's a story about pollution.

Lainie (interrupting): But it's scary—look at the beginning; everything is pretty and the cat is happy, and at the end everything is dirty.

Penny: I don't know this story, but the illustrations are fascinating; let's read the pictures.

Lainie: See, at the beginning everything is pretty and the cat is happy. It chases a butterfly. And the sky is blue.

Penny: Yes, I see how Ruth Brown [the author] begins the story with lots of bright, happy colors.

Paul: But at the end Ruth Brown uses dark colors, dirty colors.

Lainie: I think the cat looks happy at the beginning and scared at the end.

Paul: Maybe, but it is the factory that made it dark.

Penny: Wow. Great observation. The illustrations are really giving you important information. So, why do you think Ruth Brown chose those colors?

Paul: That's easy. She wanted to show us how bad these factories are.

Lainie: Right! And how unhappy the cat is.

Penny: I agree with you. She probably wanted to show how some factories can pollute the environment. Did you know that there are groups of people and organizations that work hard to control pollution from factories? Factories have rules to follow to avoid polluting the air and water. There are also people who volunteer to help with clean-up projects and work hard to keep the environment healthy.

Paul: Kids can do that, too. We pick up litter on the playground.

Mary's students are learning that illustrators, Web designers, and authors all have particular perspectives and purposes for what they design or write. Because Mary intentionally emphasizes the names of authors and illustrators, we often hear students talking about them as though they know them personally. When Penny names the author, Ruth Brown, and asks the students why they think she wrote *The World That Jack Built* or why the illustrator used color in certain ways, she is helping the children analyze the author's and illustrator's intent and learn to consider various points of view.

Discussions like these help the students become *text analysts* (see the Expanded Four Resources Model in Chapter 1 and Appendix B) who learn to recognize that their choices of words, images, and digital media make a particular point or provide a reason for taking social action. The more they learn about and analyze the power embedded in words or images, the more actively involved they become in critiquing what they read and hear, rather than merely accepting information being transmitted to them through books, video, or online media. In class discussions and project planning sessions, Mary continually reminds the students to think carefully about how they create and communicate information and share messages—to choose fonts, pictures, and colors as thoughtfully as they choose words.

🌍 The Power of Visual/Digital Communication and Expression

As part of the environment unit, the "reduce, reuse, and recycle" interest group is planning ways to raise the school's awareness of lunchroom waste. After much discussion, Sanketh, the self-proclaimed leader of the "recycle" group, suggests that they make an appointment to talk to the principal about adding recycling bins to the cafeteria. They write:

> Dear Dr. M.
> We have noticed that there is a lot of garbage in the lunchroom.
> We have been studying about ways to recycle and want to discuss some ideas with you. Can you meet with us to talk?
> > Sincerely,
> > The Recycle Group in Dr. Shorey's class

At the agreed-upon time for the meeting, Penny follows the group with the video camera to capture these social activists in action and share their presentation with the rest of the class. Sanketh, always well-prepared with information, starts the meeting, "Dr. M., we've noticed that kids are throwing their lunch garbage into one big trash barrel."

Kevin adds, "And we know that the paper, cans, and plastic need to be recycled, but there's no separate container."

Anna quietly mentions that the school lunch trays should be recycled too.

The students answer Dr. M.'s questions, and David and Kari read their research facts to him. But Dr. M. is not yet persuaded, and the students are frustrated that they didn't receive a positive answer. Feeling the need for more support, the group invites the principal to their classroom, hoping the rest of the students will help persuade him of the importance and urgency of their request. They want immediate action but are learning the importance of informed persuasion using writing, oral language, images, and technology—all the multimodal tools available to them.

Back in the classroom, their peers don't let them down. A voice from the Recycle Group says, "Dr. M., wait 'til you see the pictures we took about how much food we waste in the lunchroom. You won't believe there is so much pizza with only a bite or two out of it."

"It's in our slideshow," announces Gaby.

"And there are so many milk cartons in the garbage. I know we should recycle these," Kevin adds.

"Our group wants to do another waste-free lunch day for our whole grade," Elyana says.

"Boy, this is hard work," Natalie comments.

The children show Dr. M. their projects and lunchroom videos, which display teeming garbage cans and wasted food. Each of the groups has created reports, posters, pictures, and a slideshow to reinforce their request (see Figures 3.3 and 3.4). The students have strong, informed opinions about their topics, along with reasonable suggestions to correct the perceived problems. Taking advantage of the principal's undivided attention, they also make a case for putting healthier and more appealing food on the menu for children who purchase school lunches, as a way to reduce waste (Figure 3.5).

Unable to resist such passionate activists, Dr. M. tells the class, "I'm

Figure 3.3
The Recycle Group sorts lunchroom trash.

Figure 3.4
Naomi's Passionate Letter to the Principal

Figure 3.5
Brad and Karl
share their menu
ideas for healthier
foods and less
waste.

very impressed with what you've learned and the suggestions you are making. Your reports and well-researched documentation gave me good information, but your slideshow really convinced me that we need to do something about the student lunches. Showing me as well as telling me really helps me understand what's going on in the lunchroom and why we need to make some changes."

Following the students' lead, he gives them permission to write a letter to the school lunch program director asking for recycling bins and reusable trays. He also agrees that they can develop and distribute a survey to students about their preferred food choices, promising to consider the survey results in changing the school lunch menus.

In this "go green" experience, the students use print, visual, and digital tools to explore the environmental issues required by the curriculum. They are also learning to analyze, synthesize, and apply information from their inquiry that helps them present a knowledgeable request for action. The whole class is engaged in this experience, learning the power of persuasion from an informed perspective and the potential of visual media to enhance oral and written arguments. In addition, throughout their learning, they are also trying on the identity of environmental activists as Mary encourages them to think like scientists, develop hypotheses, ask critical questions, and brainstorm ways to help preserve a cleaner, green environment.

As an integral part of the early planning for their environmental work, students spent time discussing pros and cons of recycling and brainstorming ways to help reduce the amount of food being thrown away. Mary always refers back to the critical questions (Figure 1.2 and Appendix A) posted as anchor charts and used during read-alouds or whenever there is an opportunity to discuss perspective and point of view. The students have learned to adapt these questions to fit whatever subject is being studied. For example, environmental questions included "Whose interests are being served" by not wanting to recycle lunchroom materials? The persuasive argument they presented to the principal included the question, "Why wouldn't the school want to become a model for recycling and help teach children how to recycle in school and why they need to do this at home?" As for considering "other points of view," the children acknowledge that it would cost some money to purchase recycling garbage barrels and take more time to separate out the recyclable materials. But they believe the cost would be small compared to the positive environmental impact of recycling.

All students become passionate about subjects that are important to them. Rather than an add-on to the required curriculum, interest groups provide a way for students to collaboratively use and refine the required literacy skills (reading, writing, visualizing, using technology) while becoming experts on particular topics of their choice. Mary helps her students understand that critical inquiry also implies taking action and living their beliefs. As classroom citizen activists, they are ready and eager to make the world a more environmentally friendly place, using "go green!" as their mantra.

A Vocabulary for Design

New insights have helped us recognize the different ways that we "read" our world. When we refer to texts, we are now including digital media, Web sites, hyperlinks, visual images, illustrations, music, drama, and gestures, as well as print. These components are often used together, so we may simultaneously process images, hear music, read print, or respond to additional information in various contexts. Traditional print also requires the processing of various modalities. When we read modern communications, we pay attention to the use of fonts, white space, color, images, design of print on the page, and punctuation marks.

Today's learners have so many more ways to "read" and learn about their world than in the past. Children know how to use hyperlinks to explore a question or investigate a topic through a multitude of resources on the Internet. They are learning to use wikis and blogs and collaborate on projects through G-chats or Google Docs. They can create slideshows, videos, upload music from GarageBand, or use voice-overs to narrate a graphic novel or digital story. In addition to letter writing, pen-pal correspondence is now accomplished through e-mail, online discussions, and Skype, as students establish global connections. Online social networking is commonplace, and even young children can find a video on YouTube or connect with a friend or relative on Facebook (with parent permission, of course).

Because we are so connected to each other in new ways, critical media literacy is important to consider when using technology in the classroom. Children need to become aware of how people use language to accomplish particular purposes or use images to intentionally create a mood or evoke an emotion. Although they are still young, primary students must become critical consumers and producers of information as they begin to understand all the ways people communicate. They need to learn how to interpret the particular language or vocabulary of each literacy (particularly print, visual, and digital) as well as how and when to use them appropriately and in which contexts.

Again, we find ourselves returning to our critical questions as we teach children to use different modes of expression to accomplish their goals. We want them to use all the tools at their disposal and to move seamlessly between various modalities, but they must learn to ask the same critical questions about visual texts and Web designers that they ask about authors and illustrators of print texts. Questions such as, "What does the illustrator or designer want us to think?" Or "Whose voice is not heard?" can be used for print or images or digital information. For example, in questioning an image we can use the language of illustrators/artists/designers and ask: What techniques are used to achieve this (color, line, size, positioning)? What do you think the illustrator/artist/designer wanted the audience to know or understand? What other tools or ways of representation might be more effective?

In the earlier discussion of the book *The World That Jack Built*, the children noticed the illustrator's intentional use of color and discussed how it had helped them understand the author's intent and the story's message. Mary purposely includes comments about text illustrations and design in her think-alouds to help the students realize how they are being influenced by the visual or digital images—often together with the printed words. As they learn more about an author's intent and analyze ways to convey meaning to a reader or viewer, they are encouraged to try these techniques in their own writing or designing, becoming more proficient and articulate about explaining why they made certain decisions or how their design could impact the reader or viewer.

By carefully observing and listening to children's conversations, we notice their increased use of words and symbols unique to each literacy (e.g., *color, font, italics, design, link, Web site, perspective*). We have intentionally used these words in everyday interactions with the students to develop a shared common language that Unsworth calls a metalanguage (2002). With a repertoire of specific vocabulary for each of the different literacies, students can more clearly understand the particular modality being used and gain sophistication in constructing and conveying meaning.

For example, in Jamie's recycling drawing and paper-and-pencil report, she explains that she uses very dark letters for some of the words in her story because she wants them to be bold, as they are on the computer. The red lines underneath some of her words indicate that she thinks they might be misspelled. The italics and small pictures represent links to other information (smiley face and arrows).

To capture this emerging shared language in Mary's classroom, the students helped us create our own Language of Multiliteracies chart, which we call a Vocabulary for Design. We believe this starter list of the common, or core, vocabulary for each of the literacies is a valuable learning and communication tool to help students understand how words can be used within each of the literacies and that some terms are also interchangeable. This vocabulary gives students a way to explicitly describe their work and shows concretely how these words can be combined when designing a multiliteracies project. Knowledge of these words and the way each literacy can be used separately or together for particular purposes contributes to a clearer understanding that literacy is more than print.

We initially developed our model with just a few basic words that you can see in our Language of Multiliteracies: Vocabulary for Design chart (Figures 3.6 and 3.7 and Appendix G). As we explore each category with students, we can expand on various terms depending on the vocabulary needed for different grade levels and subjects. For example, Mary's students used a web to expand the word genre to include poetry, memoirs, historical fiction, mysteries, and so on. They may do the same with an expanded list of comprehension strategies. With the help of the technology teacher and art teacher, we will add more vocabulary to the Visual and Digital sections as the students become exposed to additional language related to those literacies (see Appendix S for additional visual and

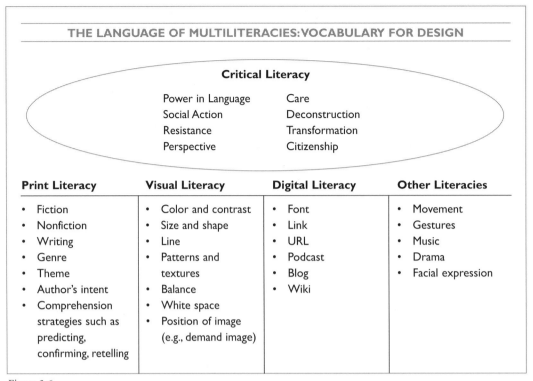

THE LANGUAGE OF MULTILITERACIES: VOCABULARY FOR DESIGN

Critical Literacy

Power in Language   Care
Social Action   Deconstruction
Resistance   Transformation
Perspective   Citizenship

Print Literacy	Visual Literacy	Digital Literacy	Other Literacies
• Fiction • Nonfiction • Writing • Genre • Theme • Author's intent • Comprehension strategies such as predicting, confirming, retelling	• Color and contrast • Size and shape • Line • Patterns and textures • Balance • White space • Position of image (e.g., demand image)	• Font • Link • URL • Podcast • Blog • Wiki	• Movement • Gestures • Music • Drama • Facial expression

Figure 3.6

Figure 3.7 Vocabulary Chart Created with Student Input

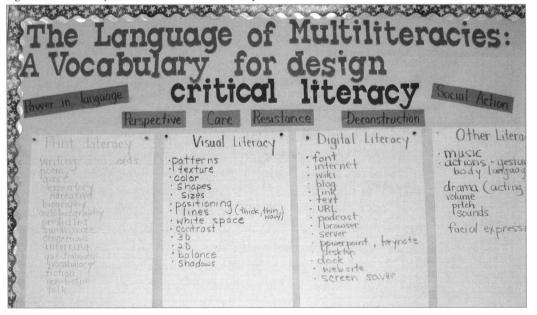

digital literacy references). It is important to note that some vocabulary is shared across categories because each of the literacies informs the others. We also wanted to represent critical literacy as an umbrella overarching all the other literacies, and while it has its own vocabulary, it is also an integral component of *all* literacies.

Being literate in the twenty-first century requires proficiency in analyzing, creating, comprehending, and using all the multimodal texts and tools that are available to learn, inform, and communicate effectively. This shared vocabulary supports the integration of multiliteracies in our teaching. Conventional print literacy continues to be a core component of many language experiences, but in addition to print instruction there must be an intentional focus on other literacies as well. The various modalities work together in unique, dynamic ways to help the "author" or "reader" construct meaning.

Visual Literacy

Students in the recycle group were intrigued with the possibilities for presenting the results of their research, using their new knowledge of visual literacy vocabulary and techniques.

"This is the ONE! We have to use this photo of the garbage spilling out of the can; just look at all that wasted food," Karl says.

"Oh, that's so gross!" Natalie agrees.

"But it really shows how much food we waste, even though pizza day is a favorite hot lunch. I don't understand why," Karl adds.

As they review the photographic evidence of the school's food waste, Ellie observes, "Look at this shot. Can you believe all these lunch trays that we took out of the garbage? It looks like they're going to fall over, the pile is so high."

"That picture should be its own slide," Karl agrees, thinking like a director. "People really need to see how much is wasted and what kids are throwing into one garbage bin."

Ellie adds, "We need to make the background black so the white trays really stand out—and put the garbage bin right in the center of the slide!"

"That sure is a 'demand photo,'" Natalie says, as the group members nod in agreement.

Ellie is passionate about making a strong statement. She and Natalie have been working on their slide, trying to find just the right size, color, and composition to influence their audience and show the significance of their visual image. Thinking creatively, Natalie suggests showing the garbage falling out of the bin with a bold red line through it—like NOT! The students are getting better at using visual and digital media to help them convey an idea or communicate the importance of an idea. They are also becoming aware of the power implied in images and design. They have a mission and recognize the impact of pictures, color, and composition on the attitudes and understanding of their viewers (audience). They know that a well-designed slide can accomplish their intent to inform the audience about the need for recycling lunchroom garbage. They have learned that the perfect demand image or just-right photograph, along with color, font, size, and positioning, can create a powerful statement to convey their message.

As elementary teachers, we have always understood the importance of encouraging students to represent meaning visually. Students continue to ask the timeless question, "Can I draw?" And of course, the answer is, "yes." Rather than seeing this as an extra or superficial part of learning, however, Mary's students know that their drawings not only support printed text, but also become a text on their own. This is reinforced when Mary emphasizes "reading the pictures" during read-alouds and encourages students to examine illustrations, images, drawings, and pictures as an important part of comprehension. They are also learning to include illustrations or images in their stories, brochures, slideshows, or videos, often combining various multimodal tools (such as music, voice-over in slides, captions for illustrations) to emphasize a particular message or present a project.

As we observe them working in their interest groups, we notice how naturally and frequently they use the vocabulary of visual design (*color, size and shape, line, patterns, texture,* and *balance*) in their conversations. The visual vocabulary, common to artists, illustrators, and designers, was once thought to be the exclusive domain of art teachers. But with an increased focus on visual literacy, it has become part of the everyday language in Mary's classroom, and we hear it being used in many learning experiences across content areas. In fact, images are assuming a place of dominance alongside—and in some cases, even surpassing—print. This is evident in the popularity of graphic novels and the proliferation of postmodern picture books (where the pictures tell a story that may or may not complement the print version). (See Appendix H for visual literacy strategies mini-lessons.)

An artist's toolbox will always include pencils, pens, brushes, paints, markers, and crayons. But in today's world those tools also include the computer with its ability to provide fonts, colors, pictures, and visual designs. Each year there are more digital resources available. Just as our students intuitively understand conventional language when learning to speak and read, digital vocabulary naturally becomes part of their vocabulary as they learn to read and interpret media (images, sound, and text).

Digital Literacy

"Dr. Silvers, listen to our sequel to *The Lorax*. I want to make a million copies, so everyone can read it," Collette calls out with her usual dramatic flair.

"No!" Naomi says, beginning to realize the power that modern communication tools provide. "We can just post it on the Web and then two million people can read it. The whole world can read it!"

"Why don't you girls just write it on the computer?" asks Penny.

"Well, we can only use the computer during our assigned time or day, so it's faster with paper and pencil," Naomi says.

"I'm taking it home tonight to type it, and then I'll send it to Dr. Shorey as an e-mail attachment," Collette confidently explains. "Then she can post it online for the whole world to see."

Naomi and Collette (Figure 3.8) began their sequel to *The Lorax* with paper and pencil but easily switched to computer-generated text, playing with colors and fonts and inserting pictures in their final copy. And of course, the grand finale was posting their sequel on the class Web page, "for the whole world to see"!

Figure 3.8
First graders create computer-generated text.

When we think about our beginning exploration of multiliteracies a few years ago, we realize that we moved from worksheets to wikis so seamlessly that it hardly seems significant. But during our first year of working together, students were only using district-approved, online programs aligned with the basal reading program. Usually these consisted of worksheets or games designed for the students to practice vocabulary, phonics, phonemic awareness, or comprehension. Many of the students wore headphones to complete their computerized, skills-based activities, and they all worked independently rather than collaboratively, letting the computer guide their learning. Over the years, the headphones have come off, students share their digital expertise with each other, and through numerous teacher demonstrations with an electronic whiteboard and presentation software, Mary now helps the students add digital literacy to their tool kit of multiliteracies as they research, inquire, compose, connect, and learn together.

Becoming Digital: Challenges and Possibilities

Digital resources present many possibilities for expanded literacy and learning. To be effective, teachers must consider new genres that may include social networking or even gaming experiences (trial and error) that are relevant to student learning. Learning how to use all these new tools is challenging for any teacher and requires a commitment to ongoing training. Mary reads professional books, consults colleagues, and attends workshops about enhancing learning through digital media. Her goal is to use these tools in meaningful ways that do more than duplicate what can be done with paper or pencil or for drill and practice. She also knows the importance of helping the students become critical consumers of information. In a journal entry she reflects on how technology is influencing her teaching:

> Digital tools are increasing, and students are talking about favorite apps along with helpful Web sites. My students have e-mail accounts, and they are using slideshows, podcasts, and videos to show their learning. My mini-lessons are changing to support this expanded view of literacy. Lessons that focus on principles of design are increasing in importance, and I frequently have discussions about Internet safety and responsible use of information. My goals are to use digital resources and to design lessons and provide opportunities for student-focused learning with technology tools.

Parents also participate in the digital process through shared conversations on a dedicated blog. The blog is presented as a tool for sharing student learning and a forum for educating parents about curriculum and instruction. Parents can initiate conversations and topics while responding to Mary and to each other. One of Mary's first threaded "e-conversations" on her blog began with this entry:

Dear Parent(s),

As the potential for using technology in the classroom and the interactive, connected features of the Internet expand, we need to consider the possibilities for our students to work and learn together even when they are not in school. Our students are already e-mailing and joining each other on approved social networks. As we learn to use technology to expand student access to information and to communicate effectively, we also need to help students learn to post and respond safely and appropriately to what is on the Internet. Please share your thoughts about some of the ways you use technology at home, guidelines for your children, and any questions you might have.

Dr. Shorey

Comment by Mr. D @ 9:00 a.m.:

With supervision, the Internet can be an amazing learning tool. Both my kindergartener and 3rd grader have access to computers at home, but only when an adult is home. In addition, we just have shortcuts to the frequented (and approved) sites on the desktops.

My child is showing more interest in exploring the District website and checking your wiki, which is fun to watch. Thanks for the new tool!!

Reply by Dr. Shorey @ 12:02 p.m.:

Thank you so much for getting this started. Our students live in a world with computers. I believe it is important to give them access from an early age and it becomes important, as you point out, to do so with supervision. Reading a website is a new genre. It isn't linear and it requires that our students be visually literate. It's both exciting and challenging!

Comment by Mrs. E. @ 7:48 p.m.:

Both of my children love using the computer. With our busy schedules during the week, they have more time on the weekend. Most of their favorite sites are ones they can access through the

District website. We also have several other "approved" sites bookmarked for them to use. My third grader is also really enjoying the school email program and loves emailing back and forth with his friends. He is gaining confidence as a writer and I like the fact that he is learning to use email in such a safe way since it's through a District enclosed system!

Comment by Mrs. H @ 9:53 a.m.:
I think this can be a great tool for the kids not only to socialize outside of school but also a great way of collaborating on homework or doing some interesting projects/research. It is always nice to see how much they learn on their own if given a chance. They can do power point presentations on various topics of their choice from Birthday cards and wish lists to phases of the moon research. It is amazing how fast they pick up skills that take so much time for adults to master.

Comment by Dr. Shorey @ 7:18 a.m.:
Dear Parent(s):
Thank you for your response on our parent Blog. Future technology plans for the students include collaborating on projects and research using our school e-mail accounts and class wiki. As you noted, the children are learning to use technology at such a rapid rate, it seems that the touch screen is as comfortable and natural to them as a pencil. Please continue to share your insights and thoughts. Thanks very much.

The social, collaborative features of digital resources are important components of today's learning environment. They provide many opportunities for sharing ongoing conversations with parents, expanding projects, and connecting students to a global community for insights, information, and even correspondence with classrooms in other countries. Just knowing that there is a vast audience for their work beyond the classroom motivates students to write more thoughtfully and edit their work more carefully. When they are able to work collaboratively with their peers, they are also learning to value each other's talents, knowledge, and insights as they make writing and production decisions to publish their work. These communication opportunities continue to evolve as we gain more experience with a variety of interactive tools and figure out new and exciting ways to use them to support student learning.

Welcome to Dr. Shorey's Wiki!

This wiki is an informational platform and a shared learning venture. We will be using our wiki throughout the year to represent both our individual thinking and collective learning. We will share writing, projects, research, and resources. We invite comments and suggestions from all visitors.

Mary began her class wiki with only a very basic understanding of how to use it and just a few ideas for projects. To get started, she encouraged the students to post samples of their stories, poems, and reports. Almost immediately, writing workshop took on a new dimension as students rushed to post their work on the wiki. They easily grasped the how-to of creating new pages, uploading photos, and displaying their work. But in the beginning, they were reluctant to take the necessary time to edit and make sure that their work was really ready for an audience. After discussing this issue with the class, Mary and the students created simple guidelines and a checklist for posting their work (see Figure 3.9 and Appendix I).

The students' enthusiasm and ability to work with the wiki surprised and amazed us. Suddenly, editing, revising, and using the cut and paste feature of digital writing were less of a chore. Although their spelling wasn't always perfect, students were looking carefully at spelling choices and eagerly using more descriptive words. Classmates such as Ethan were recognized as expert editors and called upon to help the others, giving classroom status to more students. Those students with technological expertise were particularly in demand by everyone wanting to post something on the wiki.

Of course, there were also students such as Daniel and Akshita who resisted digital writing at first. Keyboarding took a lot of time, and they weren't quite ready to post their written pieces. This was okay, too. Once a piece of writing or a drawing was edited and revised, it could be scanned and inserted onto their wiki pages, ensuring that everyone was part of the class wiki. With time and encouragement from Mary and classmates, all students eventually had postings on the class wiki.

Figure 3.9

SIMPLE RUBRIC FOR WIKI POSTS
---
1. Your work must be quality (remember the *whole world* can see it).
2. Last names may not be included on work (*Internet safety issue*).
3. Remember to edit your work before posting.

Using the wiki was exciting, but initially our focus on each student's writing was too narrow. Mary was often the only person responding to wiki postings. When other students commented, it was usually, "I like your writing" or "good work!" We needed more interactive, collaborative student involvement using the wiki. We could see that students were beginning to revise and edit their writing, often with the help of a classmate. Students loved to read each other's work, and writers looked forward to reading their classmates' comments. Now we had yet another challenge, as the comment section turned into a chat forum with remarks such as the following:

"Ellie, I love your writing!"
"Thanks, Natalie, I like yours too."
"Good job!"

It was time for a class discussion about the differences between a chat forum and comments that would support each other as writers. Mary projected student writing onto the whiteboard, and we practiced giving comments that encouraged and supported the writer, as well as suggestions for improving the written piece. Together we created guidelines and a checklist for leaving comments on the wiki page (see Figure 3.10 and Appendix J).

Monitoring the wiki and keeping up with comments is time consuming, but we considered it a trade-off or a different use of time. Instead

Figure 3.10

GUIDELINES FOR COMMENTING ON WIKI WRITING
When I view and respond to someone's work I will . . .
Support and validate their work.
Encourage them as designers and writers.
Offer helpful suggestions.
Ask questions.
Make connections with their work.
Compliment their work (I like this piece because . . .).

of editing students' writing on paper, Mary was responding to them directly on the wiki, which in itself was a learning opportunity for the children. Taking Mary's lead, the students also began responding to each other like a teacher. Through the wiki responses, they were helping their classmates become better writers and sharpening their own writing skills as well.

Despite the excitement about writing on the wiki and replying to classmates, collaborative writing proved challenging. Although students loved to work together, they were often territorial about their own writing and projects. So our class meetings and mini-lessons became demonstrations of how to write or create a project together. For example, Anthony wrote about the importance of "going green." (Anthony's original writing is in plain text; his classmate's comments are in italics.)

It is important to ***"Go Green."*** *Go green means finding ways to help the environment. It is about the 3R's: recycling, reducing, and reusing.* Everyone has to help if we want to keep the earth healthy. We have to stop polluting the earth. You can do this in lots of ways. You can remember to turn off lights, and don't throw things in water. *You can pack a reusable lunch, with containers and silverware that you can wash.* Everyone can make a difference.

We projected Anthony's writing on the screen and challenged his classmates to come up with additions to his writing and add details to enhance his great start. Emma thought we should explain what "go green" means, and she inserted the text about the three Rs and pollution. Anna added the idea about reusable lunches, and Ellie thought "Go Green" should be in a bold, green font. We shared many suggestions and used the students' writing samples for whole-class mini-lessons that focused on adding details, grammar and punctuation, summaries and closings, and other traits of effective writing. Mary also held conferences and offered guidance to meet the needs of both individuals and groups.

This sounds like a natural progression, a neat sequence for learning. In reality, it was rather messy. Some children and groups easily applied collaborative skills and worked well together. Others struggled through the process. With time and practice, students learned to build a shared report. As the students began to understand ways to create together, they also learned how to embed links to Web sites and resources. They were particularly excited to be able to link and share their individual projects (slideshows, videos, and podcasts) to the group page.

Critical Consumers and Producers

"Hey Jacob, I found some information on the whale shark. Did you know that it can float? Can I add it to your report on the wiki?" asked Eli.

"Um, I don't think so, Eli," Jacob replied.

"Now Jacob, Eli is sharing an interesting piece of information for your fact page. Remember this is a collaborative report," Mary interjected.

Jacob responded, "Well, I don't know what his source is or if it is reliable!"

"Hmm, good point," Mary said. "Eli, can you share where you got your information?" "Sure," said Eli, and the next day he brought in a book he had at home.

Jacob's response underscores the importance of Internet safety. When Mary begins a unit of study, she provides safe Internet sites that she previews and bookmarks for relevant information, organizations, links, and resources. Favorite resources include netTrekker and Encyclopaedia Britannica. Yahooligans! and Google SafeSearch are among our preferred search engines. (See Appendix K for more search tools.) Mary cautions students to pay close attention to postings that are from safe, recognizable sources. Students learn to look carefully at sources of information and ask, "How reliable is our source?" By recognizing that anyone can post information on the Internet (including students themselves), students become critical consumers of information. Inspection of sources and safe posting guidelines must be part of student learning from the first time they use the Internet (see Figure 3.11).

New digital resources continue to emerge. Two years ago, the wiki was new. Today it is commonplace in Mary's classroom. Each year presents

Figure 3.11

INTERNET SAFETY RULES
---

1. You need teacher permission to log on to the Internet.
2. Do not share your user name and password.
3. Never give out personal information.
4. Carefully select the Web sites you visit using bookmarked sites and safe search engines.
5. Do not download or install anything without checking with the teacher.

Remember Web designers are sharing their perspective and ideas. Carefully read and consider all information.

increased opportunities for expression. Mary's environmentalists began using an application called e-publishing to create books and post them into iTunes and then onto their classroom iPads. Yet, even as we learn how to use these new tools, we continually need to ask whether they help students think more deeply and enhance their lives. A critical literacy stance helps us understand that while the tools can make a difference, they are less important than the ways in which we use them. What really matters are the questions we ask using all the resources at our disposal, and recognizing the ways in which students lives are enhanced and transformed through their learning experiences.

Other Literacies

One day a group of students decided to create a skit about Karen Hesse's book *Sable*. Mary's students have always enjoyed drama, but this group of students used digital components in their planning and presentations that we hadn't anticipated. Jessie, the leader of this group, asked if they could use the electronic whiteboard screen for their scenery. They found a background of a house and projected it on the screen. Then Cam decided they could insert sound effects from a software program that is connected with the whiteboard. As we watched their skit rehearsal, we saw these savvy students using digital resources to find video clips for doors opening, dogs barking, and more. When it came time for the group to perform their creation, Mary grabbed the iTouch and videotaped the performance to be placed on the class wiki.

Through our multiliteracies research, we have expanded our understanding of traditional print literacy to include visual, digital, and critical literacies. As we observe and listen to students, we recognize that other literacies, including auditory, gestural, and spatial, all work together to create meaning: Riya sharing a YouTube video from her dance performance, the "waste-free lunch" groups posting photos on a wiki, the class discussing ways to read facial expressions and body language, Sanketh clutching a book about the history of India, or Arie using GarageBand to complete a music project about endangered whales. Mary's students are learning that meaning is embedded within and across many modes of communication. Multimodal tools help students inquire, investigate, collaborate, and share their learning, and critical literacy helps them live in the world as responsible, caring global citizens.

TEACHER TALK   *Insights & Emerging Understandings*

In today's world, curriculum and instruction must include opportunities for multimodal expression and thinking. We need to expand our understanding of literacy to include visual, digital, and other multiliteracies in addition to print. Each of these literacies has a specific vocabulary that clearly expresses the increasingly complex literacy development of today's young students. Critical literacy supports learners as they navigate a wealth of information and communication possibilities. A critical perspective is the quality that will help prepare our children to manage the demands of a technologically advanced future in the twenty-first century and beyond, to be discerning consumers of information, and to make informed decisions. A multiliteracies perspective will help them comprehend more deeply, process information more thoughtfully, and write more creatively. Simply stated, students need to be able to use a variety of resources and tools to communicate effectively.

Suggestions for using multiliteracies in your classroom:

◌ Start by developing a classroom anchor chart of vocabulary words for print, visual, and digital literacies, using the Language of Multiliteracies chart in Figure 3.6 as a resource. Discuss how the vocabulary is similar—or different—in each of the literacies.

- Like a word wall, the Language of Multiliteracies anchor chart can be started by posting just a few basic words under each category. When students notice other words (in the projects they create, class discussions, read-alouds) that are unique to different literacies, they can be added to your starter list.

◌ Ask critical questions of all text (traditional, visual, digital, musical, and gestural).

- Start with basic critical questions
  - Whose voices are heard? Whose voices are absent?
  - What does the author/illustrator want the reader to think/understand?
  - What is an alternative to the author/illustrator's message?
  - How will a critical reading of this text help me change my views or actions in relation to other people?

  Questions can be tailored to fit the needs of different subject areas and instruction. For example, in the unit on the environment, students might look at habitat destruction and ask whose voice is heard (perhaps it is the developer who is building a new shopping mall), as well as whose voice is silenced (the animals, concerned citizens). They can look at how a piece of writing or a photo is presented and how the viewer or reader may be influenced as a result: "What do you think the author/photographer wants us to think?" and "What do you think?" or "What is another way to look at this issue?" Students can also ask these same critical questions for any projects they create themselves in any subject area.

() Support, validate, and encourage multimodal communication and expression.

- When designing a unit of study or daily instruction, teachers must access and provide a variety of resources with the understanding that different modalities (visual, digital, gestural, musical) support and deepen comprehension. This may include embedding a YouTube video in a presentation lesson or finding a location for a story using Google Earth. It may mean creating flip charts that present materials visually and allow for students to interact and physically manipulate information. Or it may include saving flip charts as PDF files and posting them on the iPads for student reference. If digital resources are not available, drawing tools, music CDs, DVDs, or drama can be integrated into units and instruction.

- When students communicate their learning, they need access to multimodal tools, both print and digital.

() Remember that technology makes it possible to connect and communicate globally, and curriculum must expand as well. Today's world requires a critical perspective that recognizes and examines different points of view. Encourage students to consider the environment and use Internet resources to become informed about world events. Critical incidents that happen in the world can become meaningful, authentic ways to connect students to the world beyond the classroom and to learn to take some kind of action to help others. Use opportunities for students to analyze and critique each other's writing, Web designs, and content projects to help them become discerning interpreters of media and print information. Remember that the multimodal tools are more than a substitute for worksheets, programmed learning, or drill and practice. They are there to help students learn, communicate, and connect with others. While you may need to teach the children how to use these tools effectively or learn the terminology for various literacies, they can be powerful learning opportunities.

Favorite Books Used in Student Inquiry Projects
About the Environment
(See Appendix X for more children's text suggestions and the References at the end of this book for texts to help you use visual and digital literacies in the classroom.)

Don't Throw That Away by L. Bergen and B. Snyder
Garbage and Recycling by R. Harlow and S. Morgan
The Great Kapok Tree by L. Cherry
Just a Dream by C. Van Allsburg
Recycle! A Handbook for Kids by G. Gibbons
Reusing and Recycling by C. Guillain
The Three R's: Reuse, Reduce, Recycle by N. Roca
Weslandia by P. Fleischman
Why Should I Recycle? by J. Green
The World That Jack Built by R. Brown

Books to Highlight Visual Literacy
(See Appendix S for more text suggestions.)

Black and White by D. Macaulay
The Color of Home by M. Hoffman
Encounter by J. Yolen
Piggybook by A. Browne
The Rainbow Fish by M. Pfister
Round Trip by A. Jonas
Tar Beach by F. Ringgold
The Three Pigs by D. Weisner
Voices in the Park by A. Browne
Zoom by I. Banyai

Chapter 4

Reflective Assessment: The Bald Eagle Group

"How do you know when you are hungry?" Mary asks her young student.

Danielle, a lively and engaged first grader, grins and answers, "Well, your stomach grumbles, and that's how it tells you."

Mary continues, "How do you know you are tired?"

Danielle stifles a big yawn and replies, "You need to take a nap or lay down."

"How do you know when you are having fun?" Mary asks.

Danielle jumps up and down and replies, "You feel like laughing or running around."

Finally, Mary asks, "How do you know when you are learning?"

Danielle doesn't hesitate, "When you get a good grade."

As early as first grade, children expect tangible evidence of their learning. A grade is important, and they know it. Rather than evaluating their own accomplishments or using productive feedback from other students, they learn to look to adults for approval. Yet, at the same time, students don't usually attach much meaning to their teachers' comments, which often may not go much deeper than a smiley face or "good job."

As a first grader, Danielle had not received formal evaluations in Mary's classroom before this conference, yet somehow she knew that a "good grade" was a desirable outcome. One day, we asked Danielle to examine work samples in her portfolio and discuss how they represented her learning. She looked at each story, drawing, project, or reading log and replied, "I did a good job," but she couldn't explain how or why the papers were worthy of being in her portfolio.

At this point, we stepped in to show her. Each of us told Danielle what we saw in her work: how she had expanded her writing drafts into more detailed stories; improved her spelling on recent journal entries; used an animal research project to show she could gather information from books, pictures, captions, and Web sites and compile it into a report; and developed her reading log to include a variety of books of various genres and levels of difficulty. Danielle seemed to be listening to us, but we weren't sure our comments mattered to her.

Much to our surprise and pleasure, however, we noticed that in the weeks after our conversation Danielle began to identify some of her learning strengths and incorporate some of our evaluative, descriptive language as she explained the importance of her work. We could see that she felt more valued as a writer, reader, and student in the classroom. She also had more awareness of her growth and abilities, as well as what she could do to improve.

Like Danielle, we also continued learning and refining our understanding of how to accurately answer the question, *"How do you know when you are learning?"*

Widening Our Assessment Lens

As "kid-watchers" (Owocki and Goodman 2002), we believe it's imperative to carefully observe students in the process of learning. When we probed Danielle's thinking about her work, we helped her to "see" and reflect on her own learning. We used analogies, like those in the opening dialogue, to help her understand that she could evaluate herself without the teacher's response. This was and remains a challenging shift of focus in a system that relies so strongly on concrete, measurable data such as grades and test scores to determine merit. We've struggled for a long time to find effective and efficient ways to assess and document students' academic growth beyond standardized tests and end-of-unit exams.

Direct observations of students' learning are more important than ever in today's multiliteracies classrooms where children have so many different ways to express their understanding. We also believe that students value learning more when they are included in the evaluation process. We need to help them realize that changes in their thinking are significant indicators of their learning and just as valuable as the work they produce for the teacher to evaluate. Student self-reflection and shared goal setting go to the heart of learner-focused assessment.

Learner-Focused Assessment

To understand the challenges and the potential of this richer evaluation approach, consider the following project, which represents the culmination of a science unit Mary taught toward the end of first grade. Mary had two goals for the project. The first was focusing on an endangered animal and its habitat (required by her first-grade curriculum). Her second goal was to introduce her students to a digital presentation tool, Keynote, and explore ways to provide information both in a written format and using a variety of modalities (visual, auditory).

Working with a partner, students selected an endangered animal from a list Mary had prepared. We also gathered books and magazines and bookmarked Internet resources that students could search for information (see the "Favorite Books" section at the end of this chapter) and created a checklist with five requirements for the project, which later translated into five slides for their slideshows (see Figure 4.1).

Mary modeled ways to locate information using books and Web resources. The students worked on their organizers, but although interested

Figure 4.1

ENDANGERED ANIMAL RESEARCH CHECKLIST

Name of animal _____

☐ Describe the physical traits of your animal (size, appearance, movement, sounds).

☐ Illustrate your animal's habitat (words, pictures, and music).

☐ Discuss issues that are affecting your animal's habitat (hunting, building on land).

☐ Identify ways that your animal is being helped and ways that YOU can help it too.

☐ Design an ending slide that has a "demand" photo that creates a message for your audience.

in the animals, they were more excited about making slides on Keynote. They needed frequent reminders to focus on gathering information or finding more details instead of just playing with the technology. Before beginning the actual slideshow, we checked their information and then gave them the okay to start. The computer teacher showed the children how to navigate the slideshow program, and they created their slides with little or no help from us.

Because they were eager to try out backgrounds, fonts, colors, and transitions, we directed them back to our Language of Multiliteracies chart (see Figure 3.6 and Appendix G) to get more ideas about designing from the digital section. Soon we heard lots of conversations about when to use a bold font, the usefulness of white space, the messages that the use of color conveys, and where to place images for the greatest impact. Some students were able to add music to their slides while others stuck with simple text and a picture. Everyone was proud of the results.

We were pleased, too, noting that the students were focused on a meaningful inquiry. They were learning about habitats (a curricular expectation), and their slideshows were creative, showing emerging awareness of design and the use of technology (images) to convey a particular message. Yet, although we had the slideshow as a tangible outcome of their inquiry, we didn't have a good way of documenting the learning that had occurred through the student conversations, writing, and sharing that took place before the slides were finished. By evaluating only the final slideshow (product), we had no evidence or anecdotal observations of their thinking during the learning process.

The complex learning represented in Rachel and Lindsey's slideshow suggests the challenge:

> On Slide 1 they included a title, **The Lion**, and an image of a female lion in the wild with this description: *This is a lion. It lives in the grasslands. With its great size, the lion has a mighty voice.*
>
> **Rachel** (turning and speaking to the class): We picked this picture because it looks like she is roaring, and it shows the lion in its natural habitat.
>
> **Lindsey:** And our music sounds sort of like roaring. We wanted the audience to have a feeling for the lion, and the music creates a mood.
>
> Slide 2: **Where They Live**
> *They live in the Savanna grassland in Africa. They blend in the tall grass. They hunt carefully in the grass.*
> (music changes—softer, flowing)

Lindsey: You can hear the grass swishing and see how the grasses can protect them, especially the cubs. They almost blend into the grassy colors.

Slide 3: **Lion Issues**

The problem is that people are building on the lion's territory. We need to help save their natural habitat. How can we help the people stop building on their area? How can we keep them safe? How can we help them stay away from their enemies?

(This text is displayed on a bright red screen, and the music changes to a slower, sad tune.)

Rachel: Lions are becoming endangered all the time. They are being captured and even sent to zoos. Some zoos are okay, but many don't have the right environment to keep them healthy.

Lindsey: We need to let people know about this problem. We need to help save them from getting extinct!

Slide 4: **Helping Lions**

Some ways to help the lions are to write a note to the government. People need to stop building on their land and hunting them. And we can refuse to buy things made out of lion fur. Or you can join a wildlife group.

Slide 5: (a **photo** of a baby lion)

Lindsey and Rachel (turning to face the audience directly): We need to help this lion and others like it. We put it in the middle of the slide to get your attention. What can we do to help?

Their classmates were clearly moved by the presentation as they responded with an audible medley of, "Oh, how cute," "How sad," and "She needs our help." The girls asked if there were any questions, and their classmates engaged in an animated discussion of other animals that are endangered and what they could do to help.

As teachers we were struck by the girls' sophisticated treatment of the topic and the simplistic way that we had originally planned to evaluate their learning. For example, we thought it was important to note how and why Lindsey and Rachel had decided which pictures to use with the slides, the reason for their music choices, and their emerging understanding of the economic reasons that lions were becoming endangered. We also thought our observations of the students' collaboration and inquiry processes held additional meaning that couldn't be captured in a typical project rubric. We wanted some way to hold onto that thinking as part of the overall assessment of the students' learning throughout this unit.

So it was back to the drawing board. Our teacher discussions helped us realize that so much learning goes on right under our eyes, but it often goes unnoticed because we don't know to look for it. We are so accustomed to assessing the end product that we tend to dismiss or ignore the in-process thinking as less important than the final outcome. To us it now made sense to design an assessment that would include observations of what students were doing and thinking throughout their learning so we could highlight the changes from beginning to end. We also wanted to include them in the process of self-assessment along with the assessment received from the teacher.

To do this, we needed explicit guidelines to help the students make their learning visible. The first-grade endangered animal checklist included criteria for sharing research about the chosen animal. We intended to challenge students' thinking by asking them to apply what they had learned from their research in the design of their slides. We also wanted the information on the slides to help viewers understand how the animals were nearing extinction and create a desire to help make a difference on behalf of the animal. But we still needed ways for students to assess their own learning and set goals from start to finish (process to product). We wanted students to understand that learning involves more than just gathering and repeating facts. This metacognitive process, thinking about their thinking, is an important step for all learners, including six-year-olds.

In addition to discovering a better way to evaluate students' thinking and collaboration, we were intent on finding ways to document how they used various tools, communicated information, and created compelling presentations that "spoke" to the audience. From the beginning, we had stressed to students that they should be keenly aware of the *audience* for their projects, recognizing that they were presenting a particular message to intentionally influence people through the use of words, images, and design.

After many discussions, observations, and experiments, we came up with criteria that support our expanded vision of literacy and learning. This assessment model didn't come to fruition during that first-grade year when students completed endangered animal slideshows, nor the next year as we continued to revise our checklists and rubrics. But the following year when Mary returned to teaching third grade, we were ready to pilot a model. We were informed by experience, research, and reading. But it really was the children, especially four inquiring minds known as the Bald Eagle Group, who helped us refine the model and demonstrate its effectiveness.

🌍 Capturing the Learning Process: An Assessment Framework

Our assessment model provides a system of accountability for nonstandardized and process data and offers a way for teachers to incorporate anecdotal observations and insights about their students' thinking (see Figure 4.2 and Appendix L). It captures students' use of multimodal tools, understanding of critical questions, and developing sense of social justice. It reveals deeper learning by highlighting ways they are applying the content rather than just putting a grade on a completed project. The model also supports and provides evidence of student choice, diversity, collaboration, and creative design of their final products. Most importantly, it facilitates student reflection and self-evaluation and a deeper sense of their own identity as citizens who can—and should—make a difference in the world.

Although the model may look complicated, the same six categories are repeated throughout the three phases of the learning cycle: Planning, Involvement, and Evaluation. Students and teachers can use the model to design and assess their applications of learning. The categories can be expanded or revised to meet many different curricular expectations and everyday learning needs. Let's take a closer look at the components:

Phase 1: Planning

We need to help students realize that the first step in any project or learning experience is planning and organizing their work.

Students begin by identifying the **content** (topic, subject) they will be investigating or learning about. They activate their prior knowledge and enter into the learning experience through an inquiry or question, clarifying what they need or want to know. Moving through the categories, students can think about their learning purpose or **intent** and the significance of what they are accomplishing. A focus on **audience** helps students understand that every activity or assignment, writing, illustration, or Web design is created (authored) by someone with a particular purpose, focus, or perspective. The understanding of a larger audience—whether classmates, parents, other children, teachers, or people in the community beyond the school—provides an authentic context and motivation for effective communication and creative completion of the project. Thinking about

ASSESSMENT MODEL FOR TWENTY-FIRST-CENTURY LEARNING			
	PHASE 1	**PHASE 2**	**PHASE 3**
	Planning	*Involvement*	*Evaluation of Learning*
Content	• What is your topic or subject? • What do you already know, and what questions will you ask? • How will you organize your learning?	• Is your information focused? • How are you gathering your information? • Are you using multiple resources?	• Is your assignment focused on topic? • Do you have detailed information? • Have you cited your resources?
Intent or Purpose	• What is the purpose or intention of this work? • How can this engagement make a difference in some way?	• Is the purpose clear? • Are multiple perspectives being considered?	• Does this artifact fulfill its purpose?
Audience	• Who is the audience for this work? • Who else might be interested?	• Is there awareness of audience? • Is it clear who the audience is or may be?	• Is it appropriate for the intended audience? • Who else might be interested?
Composition/Design	• What tools are needed? • Is the plan realistic? • Is the desired outcome clear? • What resources will be used? • How will this learning be shared?	• Are there a variety of tools and resources being used? • Are critical questions being asked? • Is the new vocabulary being applied?	• Did the tools and resources accomplish the desired effect? • Is the artifact focused and organized? • Does it include a variety of modalities?
Social Action	• Can you make real-life connections? • Is there an awareness of a need to make a difference?	• Are different outcomes being explored? • Are possibilities for social action being considered?	• Does the artifact make a difference/fulfill its purpose? • Is there potential for appropriate social action?
Reflection	• What were my thoughts/ views when I started?	• What do I now know (understand, realize)? • What difference does this make to me? • How did this experience change my thinking/ understanding?	• What new questions do I have from this experience? • How am I different? • How did this expand my understanding of multiliteracies to convey and communicate something meaningfully? • Did this make a difference for others and for myself?

Figure 4.2

audience also reminds students that the teacher is not the only one who will see and evaluate their work. It guides students as they monitor their choice of words and images and recognize how these become part of the larger text and purpose.

Awareness of **composition/design** requires students to consider the wide range of tools and multimodal choices available to demonstrate and share the learning. It also asks students to pay attention to principles of design such as effective use of line, color, space, and appropriate fonts. **Social action** reminds students to consider the significance of their learning both for themselves and for others. It challenges them to respond to information, to analyze its implications, and to think about ways to use that information to make a difference. Finally, **reflection** serves as a reminder that the ultimate goal of assessment is helping students take responsibility for their own learning, to acknowledge their changes and growth.

Phase 2: Involvement

During the learning process, both students and teachers need to monitor student involvement and engagement in the learning experience. It is important to document the students' use of various tools (anecdotal notes, reflections, journals, video, audio, artifacts) and the development of metacognitive thinking about their learning. In this phase we observe how the learning is progressing; content is being explored; what tools, information, or practice is needed; and the extent of student understanding about different perspectives, audience, application of critical questions, problem solving, consideration of possibilities for taking social action, and collaborative participation with classmates.

Phase 3: Evaluation of Learning

In this third phase, students and teachers, individually and together, consider whether or not the outcome, artifact, or final product has fulfilled its purpose. Throughout the learning engagement, students have been using all six categories to inform and assess their process. At this final stage we can reflect on the overall experience in order to ask new questions, analyze the significance, and consider the outcomes. Of great importance is the final reflection that asks the children to consider what they learned; what new questions might have emerged; how their use of print, technology, and images expanded their understanding of the topic and the communication process; and how this experience might have been transformational or made a difference for the student and the intended audience (some change in behavior or social action as an outcome of the learning).

These three phases represent a recursive process: we keep moving through them at deepening levels of learning, engagement, and self-reflection. By intentionally raising students' awareness of where they are in the process, we can teach them how to evaluate what they are doing and how well, using that knowledge to make informed decisions about what they need to do next to move their learning forward.

The Bald Eagle Group

The Bald Eagle group was the first to try out our assessment model. The group members were very passionate about their topic and found many opportunities to work together during lunch and even after school, in addition to classroom work time (see Figure 4.3). They were eager to share their information with the class and very willing to meet with us to discuss ways to capture and assess their learning. The design and application of this model evolved through the diligent work of the students.

Planning

"Dr. Shorey, look at all these books I found on the bald eagles, and I did some writing," Jenny announces as Mary joins their group. "Adam, Caleb, and Karen have resources, too. We are excited to get started."

"It looks like you already have," Mary replies, acknowledging the collection of materials already present on the table. "I can't wait to learn about this important topic."

Figure 4.3
The Bald Eagle
Inquiry Group

Jenny had been a student in Mary's first-grade classroom two years before, so she was familiar with the inquiry process. She and three classmates became interested in the bald eagle population after hearing on the news that two baby eaglets had fallen from their nest during a violent thunderstorm and were being cared for by forest preserve officials. Recognizing the importance of the rescue and the need to return the eaglets to the wild, the students conducted research to see if they could help in some way. As they learned about the bald eagle, they became fascinated with its history and status as our national emblem. They also discovered that while bald eagles have been removed from the official endangered species list, their habitats are still threatened. They felt strongly that everyone needs to be involved in preserving the eagles. Figure 4.4 highlights the questions that guided the students through the early discovery stages. The Bald Eagle Group became the test pilot for our new assessment model.

Figure 4.4

ASSESSMENT MODEL, PHASE I: PLANNING	
PHASE I	
Planning	
Content	• What is your topic or subject? • What do you already know, and what questions will you ask? • How will you organize your learning?
Intent or Purpose	• What is the purpose or intention of this work? • How can this engagement make a difference in some way?
Audience	• Who is the audience for this work? • Who else might be interested?
Composition/Design	• What tools are needed? • Is the plan realistic? • Is the desired outcome clear? • What resources will be used? • How will this learning be shared?
Social Action	• Can you make real-life connections? • Is there an awareness of a need to make a difference?
Reflection	• What were my thoughts/views when I started?

"Your subject or **content** is the bald eagle," Mary explains, referring to the first category on the organizer. "You can begin with anything that you already know about these eagles and write out or record this data. Then you can ask questions to guide your research and learning. Remember to organize your information. You will also need to think about **intent** and ask yourself, 'What is my purpose? How can I clearly describe it?'"

Jenny jumps in, interrupting Mary, "For your **audience**, what good is it if you do a lot of reading, researching, writing, and have no one pay attention to it?"

Mary nods and continues, "So who do you think is the audience for your work?"

The students are silent for a minute, deep in thought.

"Well, I think it is our classmates," Karen answers.

"Yes," Adam agrees, "the class needs to see that there is a problem."

"So they want to get involved, you know, to help," Caleb continues the line of thought.

"And when we put our information on the wiki, more people can see it, and we hope they will do something," Jenny adds.

Impressed with their responses, Mary tells the students, "Good thinking—you have identified the next two categories on our checklist, **intent**, and **audience**. I like how you began by identifying our class as the first audience and then expanding this audience in a global way through the wiki."

When Mary mentions **composition/design** as the next category, Karen can't wait for the full explanation. "Oh, this is the category that I love," she adds. "You get to make slideshows, movies, projects. It's the creative part, and I'm good at this, but I wasn't always good at it. When I first learned to make slideshows that is all I wanted to do. I only focused on pictures, music, transitions, and I sort of forgot about using good information."

As Karen recalls her progress in understanding that creativity must be paired with substantive facts and content, other students quickly share examples of their learning.

"Remember how I highlighted everything in my first interest group project?" Adam asks.

"Oh, right," Caleb says, "and I had to do my tropical fish page all over again because I just copied information. I made the real author's words my own, and I had to rewrite everything to make it my own words."

"This part is so important," Jenny says, reflecting on the rubric. "We have to make our home page really work for us. It is the first thing that the audience will see on the wiki. We need to grab their attention and direct them to our special topic pages" (see Figure 4.5).

Figure 4.5
Introduction to
the Wiki Page for
the Bald Eagle
Group

By: Jenny, Karen, Caleb and Adam pes3shorey10
You've found the BALD EAGLE page!:Explore the wonderful world of Bald Eagles!!!
On this page you will be learning about the Bald Eagle! They are endangered and we
want you to help them! Learn about their appearance, habitat ,ways to help, how they
are endangered and more! When you are done reading this page we hope you make a
difference in the Bald Eagle's life!

Bald Eagles

Caleb adds, "I'm already thinking that maybe a picture would be a good grabber, you know, like a demand image."

"Um, I think it should be some exciting facts . . . you know the kind that makes you think, 'tell me more,'" Adam interjects. "Oh, and our work must be organized."

Mary smiles, pleased that her students understand the expectations for each category. "Good thinking, group. Keep talking about that home page. It's sort of like a table of contents. Let's take a look at the interest group project organizer. I think this may be a good starting place." (See Figure 4.6 and Appendix M.)

"We're already using it," Jenny quickly replies. "That's why I brought in books, and you have already approved our topic."

"I like it because it's only one page long," says Adam. His peers nod in agreement.

Mary uses variations of this project sheet for interest group research throughout the year. It serves as an organizer for both student and teacher accountability, highlighting the students' processes as they work. Because it is both basic and expansive, the project sheet enables Mary to differentiate instruction and assessment. For example, Jenny may complete her report quickly, easily navigating through the project's checkpoints, and she may do several choice projects independently. Caleb's reading comprehension and writing abilities are not as developed as Jenny's, but he can meet the minimum requirements and will benefit from teacher guidance during the checkpoints.

"You seem to have a clear understanding of **content, intent, audience, and composition and design**," Mary continues. "The next category is **social action**. The question it asks is, 'How can I use my learning to make a difference for myself and others?' Can you describe how you will plan for social action in your research and project? Jenny, do you remember when

---

INTEREST GROUP ORGANIZER

Name: _____

1. Select a topic. _____

2. Who may be interested in your topic? _____

3. Who will you work with? _____

Have your topic approved by the teacher. _____

4. What resources do you need . . . books, Web sources? _____

_____

Gather resources…

5. Brainstorm questions to guide your research (attach these).

Share your questions with the teacher. _____

6. Write a **collaborative** report and discuss *why* your report is important. Will it help endangered animals in some way?
   a. Discuss the design of your report with your group members.
   b. Share the writing.
   c. Pay attention to presentation.
      i. Did you capture the BIG ideas?
      ii. Is it edited?
      iii. Is it your best effort? A quality project?

Have your report monitored and checked by the teacher. _____

7. **Individual or group project(s).** These may be started after your group report is near completion.
   a. You may do more than one project, but you must have information and details gathered before you can put your information into a display.
   b. You need to pay attention to the design of your project—we will discuss design principles and ways to make your project work.

Have your project monitored and checked by the teacher. _____

Figure 4.6

you did a slideshow on the polar bear when you were in my first-grade room? I believe that project was a starting place for you as you learned about ways to make a difference."

Jenny happily describes that project, "Sure, I picked the polar bear because its habitat was disappearing. I remember it was because of global warming."

The group members listen intently to Jenny as she describes how she picked photos and put them into her project to show the problem. It was the first time that she had used music in a slideshow.

"Wow, you did that in first grade?" Karen asks admiringly.

"We all did," Jenny says. "We were looking for ways to help. We even adopted a gray fox when we went on our field trip to the zoo."

Mary proceeds to connect the students' comments to the next assessment frame, "Yes, I believe that social action means doing something with your learning. It might be just helping our class be aware of a need to do something."

Adam adds, "Right, in our report we need to make the problem very clear so the audience will think about how they can help."

Karen continues, "I'm already thinking about organizations that can help the bald eagle. When I was in first grade, I adopted a zoo animal, too. But I remember I was more interested in the free stuffed animal, and now I can see that it is more than that. I mean, you have to clearly understand that you are doing something for the animals that really need help."

Mary again redirects the students' powerful insights to the assessment framework. "You know Karen, Jenny, Adam, and Caleb, when you think about your learning over time, like we are doing right now, you are reflecting. That's the last category on our assessment checklist: **reflection**," she says. "It is probably the most important category. As lifelong learners, myself included, it is so important to think about your thinking . . . doesn't that sound funny? We must always be asking ourselves questions like, 'What am I learning? Why am I learning this? What do I know now that I didn't know or understand before? What questions do I have? I wonder . . . what if . . . what's another way to look at this?' And when you finish a project does the learning stop?"

"I don't think so," replies Adam, following Mary's lead. "I mean, you can always add more information. It's easy to do on a wiki page."

"Yes," Karen agrees, "my project on nutrition is still growing, like when we read about Mrs. Obama and her work with school lunch programs."

"Good example," Mary answers. "And I hope, boys and girls, that you will always ask questions . . . reflection means understanding that learning

Figure 4.7

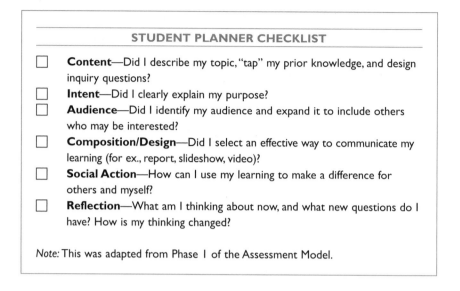

never stops. It means that you need to take the time to really think about what you are learning and challenge yourself to do more or sometimes to even redo or rework an activity, project, or lesson."

Jenny adds, "Yes, and Dr. Shorey, you know we're on the wiki even when we're not in school. We can add new facts anytime."

"Right," says Mary. "Now, let's get started."

These insightful third graders demonstrated that they can understand and engage in thoughtful, reflective assessment. They reminded us that it is important to discuss our expectations with students and to check frequently for understanding. After this initial conversation we created a simple planning checklist that captured the BIG ideas for each assessment category and had students post these on their research folders for easy reference (see Figure 4.7 and Appendix N).

Involvement

Phase 2 of the assessment model is designed to inform and capture the learning process. This is the part of the engagement that is usually most difficult to make concrete enough to assess (see Figure 4.8). To help us understand how to do this, we carefully watched all of Mary's third graders as they used the assessment model to guide their learning during interest group work, paying particular attention to the Bald Eagle Group. The Bald Eagle Group met when students had independent work time during Mary's afternoon literacy block, sometimes gathering at a back table to

Figure 4.8

ASSESSMENT MODEL, PHASE 2: INVOLVEMENT	
PHASE 2	
Involvement	
Content	• Is your information focused? • How are you gathering your information? • Are you using multiple resources?
Intent or Purpose	• Is the purpose clear? • Are multiple perspectives being considered?
Audience	• Is there awareness of audience? • Is it clear who the audience is or may be?
Composition/Design	• Are there a variety of tools and resources being used? • Are critical questions being asked? • Is the new vocabulary being applied?
Social Action	• Are different outcomes being explored? • Are possibilities for social action being considered?
Reflection	• What do I now know (understand, realize)? • What difference does this make to me? • How did this experience change my thinking/understanding?

work together. Other times, the students would assign tasks to each member and work independently. Sometimes they asked to stay in for recess to continue their research. They were motivated and enthusiastic, and their learning process was rich with anecdotal information.

Jenny: Let's check in and see what we've done. I've been busy researching organizations that help bald eagles. I even created a link to one that I think is really good.

Caleb: And I've been working on our home page. Did you see our home page? I added lots of pictures. And did you see that we have sections—you know sort of a table of contents?

Adam: Right, we thought we'd only have four sections: appearance, habitat, why they are endangered, and how to help—but we had too much information, so I added two other categories, predators and information. I like the opening paragraph, and I think it helps the audience see that they need to read about the bald eagle. I also think we need more information about their habitat, and I am thinking, Caleb, that you might have too many pictures.

Karen: I disagree! I think Caleb's photos really tell a story. When I look at that photo of the sick eagle, it really helps me understand how chemicals in the environment can harm them. And I love the photo on the first page. The eagle looks so beautiful!

Using notes to track the students' participation, Mary and Penny notice how Jenny has taken on a leadership role in the group. They note her strong sense of intent and a need for action. She is a good editor who reviews and edits the group's work regularly. Anecdotal comments about Karen refer to her thoughtful explanation of the design process. She often talks about the overall visual appeal of the project, referencing choice of photos, color, or placement of figures on a page. Adam asks lots of questions, playing devil's advocate as he challenges his teammates to justify the content they want to include. He is also very aware of audience and often refers to this category. For example, he was critical of the home page and wondered if it was distracting, thinking it did not offer enough information about the eagle's habitat. Other times he was very concerned about the organization of the group's report and proper citation of resources. Caleb is a thoughtful contributor, very visual in his presentation, and exceptionally skilled at using technology. He is the "how-to" student, proficient and helpful at adding photos, creating links, and posting on the wiki.

We sometimes jotted down these student observations while in the process of meeting with the group, but more often we would make notes when we reflected on how the project was progressing. Audio recordings helped us preserve data. The students enjoyed these conversations, often taping them on their own. Playing them back opened up opportunities for students to reflect on their contributions and notice their evolving thinking. Occasionally, we set up a Flip camera and watched the student interactions in addition to listening to what they were saying.

One day Penny joined the group, and they were very eager to share their progress. "Dr. Silvers, check out our wiki. We have been adding lots of pages," Karen said excitedly. The children quickly navigated to their home page and proudly displayed their new pages, pictures, and links to information. "Wow, you have really designed this home page well," Penny shared, matching the enthusiasm of the group. "I like how you have subject categories. Your opening paragraph is inviting, and you have clearly

Welcome to Room 24's Wiki

Welcome to Dr. Shorey's Wiki!

This wiki is an informational platform and a shared learning venture. We will be using our wiki throughout the year to represent both our individual thinking and collective learning. We will share writing, projects, research, and resources. We invite comments and suggestions from all visitors.

These are questions we discussed as we began...

- What make wiki websites different from other websites?
- What is the most well-known wiki?
- Who gets to see what is published on wiki?

We recognize that wikis are great ways to share information we know with others and to learn together. We just need to remember to use it responsibly!

Figure 4.9 Class Wiki Welcome Page

WIKI TABLE OF CONTENTS

Subjects:

Habitat

Appearance

Predators

Endangered animal

Who has helped

How you can help

Figure 4.10 Wiki Table of Contents

---

shown your intent. You write like you are talking to your audience, and you plant the idea that everyone needs to become involved and help the bald eagle. Your pictures are excellent. Let's look at each of the subject pages you have started and the links you have on your home page—see what more you need. You might want to make some notes to identify edits, add more details, or to remember what you want to talk about." (See Figures 4.9 and 4.10 for wiki excerpts.)

Because both the teacher and students are continuously monitoring the inquiry project with the student planner checklist, we often use whole-class mini-lessons to target specific categories in the assessment model. For example, the start of student work time would include lessons or tips on how to organize information, add details, cite sources, or create links to organizations that support various interests. Other times, we would provide direct instruction in response to the needs of individual interest groups.

"Dr. Shorey, we want to make an infomercial, like we did for our Simple Machine Unit [referring to an assessment project they did in science]," Jenny informs Mary as the group begins planning for Phase 3, the evaluation or final product of their learning.

"We think it would be a great way to show how important it is to help bald eagles," adds Karen.

Figure 4.11

INFOMERCIAL CHECKLIST

_____ Topic

_____ Information

_____ Message

_____ Action Plan

_____ Script draft

_____ Edit

_____ Final Draft

_____ Rehearse

_____ Videotape

_____ Edit in iMovie

_____ Publish and share

"We can have music and powerful pictures," Caleb says.

"And maybe we can include sites for people to use to make donations," says Adam.

"That's an interesting idea; I think it would be a good 'grabber' and you can use the checklist we created for our Simple Machines infomercials to get you started. I can't wait to see what you design," Mary responds. Figure 4.11 shows the infomercial checklist that the students used (also provided in Appendix O).

Evaluation of Learning

It takes about two weeks for the Bald Eagle Group to write a script. The students use their planning checklist to make sure they address all areas, including an explanation of how the bald eagle has been placed on the watch list for endangered animals. Their intent is clearly demonstrated, and they appeal to both an audience of their classmates and a broader audience beyond school that they could reach with their wiki. The group shares and edits their scripts with us. They plan for Mary to videotape their performance during lunch. On the day of the taping they sit cross-legged on colorful beanbag chairs. Each student has made a paper eagle they have taped to one of their shoulders and memorized their lines. Their presentation shows both their passion and strong focus on social action.

Karen: The bald eagles are fascinating animals, but they are threatened. I'm wondering how we can help them.

Jenny: I've been wondering the same thing, too. Could I do anything to help?

Adam: Yes, you can. There are simple things you can do to help the bald eagle.

Caleb: I think you can tell people around you not to shoot the bald eagle. Then you raise awareness.

Adam: Bald eagles are our national symbol, so I think we should protect them, too.

Karen: I will do that!

Jenny: How else can we help the bald eagle?

Caleb: We also need to respect the bald eagle's home, so we should not destroy its shelter.

Karen: That sounds so easy!

Adam: Yes, there are many ways to help.

Jenny: One important way is to donate money to organizations that help bald eagles.

Their commercial is about two and a half minutes long, and by the time it is taped and published to the wiki, the group is also ready to present it to their classmates. They decide to first show their video to the class and then highlight pages on the wiki. The group is relentless, continually stressing the importance of really doing something to help this cause. In the video they tell the audience that every dollar donated helps and explain simple math (for example, if everyone donated one dollar it would be . . .). When sharing with their peers, they challenge them by asking, "Do you think you can donate something?" And the enthusiastic audience responds, "Yes!"

With that, all eyes turn to Mary, and the unspoken questions are, *How? Now what?* Hands raise, and students begin saying, "My mom will give five dollars," or "I can give one dollar," or "Maybe we can sell cookies." Mary quickly jumps in and replies, "Well, we'll have to explore this a bit. I'll meet with the Bald Eagle Group and discuss how this might work. Remember, just a couple of weeks ago we raised money for bracelets for Japan [a school fundraiser], and I think it's great that you want to help, but let's think this over a bit."

We called a meeting of the Bald Eagle Group to discuss what to do about donations. Together we examined the Web site they had found to see if it was a legitimate place to contribute money. Mary had an idea, and she gently guided her students to consider an option that wouldn't cost the parents more money. She reminded the students that at the beginning of the year, each one had brought in $3.25 in coins to use for math when practicing how to count money. Because it was the end of the year, these coins would be returned to the students. When Mary mentions this, Jenny immediately responds, "Yes, I remember in first grade we used our math coin money to adopt the gray wolf. We can do the same thing this year but send the money in to help the bald eagle!"

"Do you think your classmates would like to donate this cash?" Mary asks, and when the Bald Eagle Group unanimously agrees, Mary reminds them: "Donations are voluntary. We should ask students if they would like to do this and then inform parents about this project. I'd like your group to draft a letter for students and families explaining this project idea."

The students get to work at the back table. Fifteen minutes later, they present a completed letter. "This is the one we picked," says Jenny. "We each wrote a letter and voted on the one we wanted. Here it is" (see Figure 4.12).

Figure 4.12

STUDENT-GENERATED DONATION LETTER

June 3, 2011

Dear Families,

We have been doing an interest group about the Bald Eagles. We have a wiki page about them, and today we showed the page to the class. We have been trying to help them, but we need your help. On Monday our class will get their math coins back that we used to practice counting money this year ($3.25). If they want to donate their money to Http://www.eagles.org/donate.php, fill out this form and bring it back on Monday.

Thank you,
Jenny, Caleb, Karen, Adam
The Bald Eagle Group

- -

Please fill this out if you want to help.
☐ Yes   ☐ No
Student Name _____

The Bald Eagle Group members share their idea with their classmates and then ask for a vote. The majority of students vote in favor of donating their math coins to the bald eagle cause. We sent the letter home and subsequently raised seventy-five dollars for the bald eagle's preservation. With an excited smile on her face Karen announces, "We really did it. We helped the bald eagle!"

Afterward, when we realized how well the students had navigated through the final phase of our assessment model, we wondered if we should create another rubric to evaluate the finished product with descriptors that would match Mary's report card criteria. The school district's grades, from lowest to highest, were AC—Academic Concern, D—Developing skills, M—Meets grade-level expectations, and E—Exceeds grade-level expectations. Recognizing the difficulty of distinguishing among the criteria within the categories, we tried to include some more descriptors (see Figure 4.13). It was better, but still not ideal.

When we showed the rubric to the Bald Eagle Group for productive feedback or suggestions, the group confirmed some of our concerns about the imperfect rubric.

Figure 4.13

PROJECT EVALUATION					
	Area of Concern	**Learning**	**Meets**	**Exceeds**	**Self**	**Teacher**
	1 pt.	2 pts.	3 pts.	4 pts.		
Content (Subject) Objective	• Topic is unclear • Sketchy information • Lacking resources	• Most information is on topic • May need more information • Two to three resources cited correctly	• Focused on topic • Required information is provided • Three resources correctly cited	• Focused on topic • Detailed information • Many resources cited correctly		
Intent	• Unclear purpose • Incomplete	• Purpose is identifiable, but focus is not maintained	• Purpose is identified, • Effective introduction and conclusion	• Purpose is explored • Insightful, detailed introduction and conclusion		

Jenny: Well, I think that the component that was most important for me was social action. It is so cool that our class is going to actually donate money to help bald eagles.

Adam: I think that we had a lot of information, and the content of our project was organized and very detailed.

Caleb: Our project was creative. The infomercial was so much fun.

Karen: That's composition and design that you are talking about Caleb. And I agree with you.

Jenny: I think the next time that we do this we should invite the class to ask us questions at the beginning, the middle, and the end.

Caleb: And they could add their own information, too.

Mary: I like the way you are talking about the different components of the planning checklist. Do you feel that filling out a rubric would be helpful?

Jenny: Um, Dr. Shorey. We don't really need to do that. We have been filling out the rubric all the time we have been working.

Penny: Perhaps what you could do is write about what you felt went well, any challenges that you had, new questions, etcetera—a reflective piece.

Along with the students, we recognized the redundancy in asking them to fill out a rubric that matched what they had been doing all along. At this point in the project, the boys and girls had already internalized the evaluation components. When they reflected on their finished project, they recognized their individual interests, strengths, and contributions. They also knew that together they had created an excellent project. They didn't see a need to give a point value to each part of the rubric, but they did understand the importance of reflection. And so we added a column to Phase 3 of the Assessment Model and asked them to reflect on their final production. Figure 4.14 shows this addition (a blank template is provided in Appendix P). Figures 4.15 and 4.16 show the students' comments.

Interestingly, each member of the Bald Eagle Group commented on how well they had worked together. We discussed the possibility of adding participation as a category, but it seemed that when students understand and take ownership of a learning engagement, collaboration and participation are natural expectations. That is not to say that it works smoothly every time. We know that some groups are more challenging than others, but by making collaboration an expectation, discussing progress along the way, sharing tasks, and celebrating every contribution, we can support this group work. As we reflected on this final phase of our model, we could now see that an added rubric wasn't necessary.

ASSESSMENT MODEL, PHASE 3: EVALUATION OF LEARNING

PHASE 3

	Evaluation of Learning	Student Reflection
Content	• Is your assignment focused on topic? • Do you have detailed information? • Have you cited your resources?	I really learned a lot about our National Emblem. I also learned about the issues that connect with endangerment. We had a lot of resources.
Intent or Purpose	• Does this artifact fulfill its purpose?	Yes
Audience	• Is it appropriate for the intended audience? • Who else might be interested?	My class was interested, so are my parents, maybe the whole world!
Composition/Design	• Did the tools and resources accomplish the desired effect? • Is the artifact focused and organized? • Does it include a variety of modalities?	I think doing an infomercial was a great way to share information along with the slideshows and the solid report.
Social Action	• Does the artifact make a difference/fulfill its purpose? • Is there potential for appropriate social action?	I liked the social action. I think people will really want to help the Bald Eagle and I think they will!
Reflection	• What new questions do I have from this experience? • How am I different? • How did this expand my understanding of multiliteracies to convey and communicate something meaningfully? • Did this make a difference for others and for myself?	We might keep coming back and posting more information. I really think our donations will make a difference.

Additional comments: I had fun getting involved in doing something good for the earth and working together was something I liked and needed to work on.

Figure 4.14

Figure 4.15
Caleb's Bald Eagle
Inquiry Reflection

I really liked how the bald eagle group worked. We really learned a lot about the Bald eagle. How you share your work is an important thing to think about too. I think doing an infomercial was a great way to share information along with the slideshows and the solid report. I really liked how our group worked together to try to make a Page that could Save our national symbol the bald eagle.

Figure 4.16
Jenny reflects on
the Bald Eagle
inquiry project
and assessment.

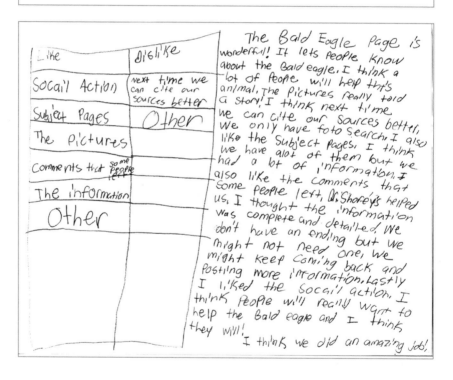

Like	Dislike
Socail Action	next time we can cite our sources better
Subject Pages	Other
The Pictures	
Comments that some people left	
The information	
Other	

The Bald Eagle Page is wonderful! It lets people know about the Bald eagle. I think a lot of people will help this animal. The Pictures really told a story! I think next time we can cite our sources better. We only have foto search. I also like the Subject pages. I think we have alot of them but we had a lot of information. I also like the comments that some people left us. I thought the information was complete and detailed. We don't have an ending but we might not need one, we might keep coming back and Posting more information. Lastly I liked the Socail action. I think people will really want to help the Bald eagle and I think they will!
I think we did an amazing job!

This assessment model can really be adapted endlessly. For example, you could add participation as a category in each of the three phases. You could also add a point value to Phase 3 to satisfy district grading requirements. Different categories in the rubric could be emphasized depending on the goals of the learning engagement. For example, a first-grade research project like Rachel and Lindsey's slideshow on animal habitats might require a strong emphasis on **content** as students learn beginning research skills. A booktalk about a realistic fiction book may have a strong emphasis on **audience**. When students select the best way to share information, they may focus on **composition/design**. Every engagement addresses each category, but the emphasis may shift. When students look at author's purpose or **intent** (including their own), they challenge themselves to search for evidence of or possibilities for **social action**, and throughout the learning engagement students are using **reflective** language as they self-assess and take ownership of the learning process. Regardless of the activity, the model can help all of us (teachers and students) see, experience, and capture the process of thinking, collaborating, and making decisions. There will always be core content to learn, but students today must also know how to access, synthesize, and evaluate information.

The process of learning is as important—if not more important—than the final product or project that demonstrates learning outcomes. This assessment model makes the students' learning process visible and documents it in a way that everyone can understand. It validates self-assessment and process observations and provides accountability for student learning of content, as well as deep thinking and reflection. It gives students ownership of their learning, choices of topics, ways to engage in inquiry, and opportunities to take some kind of action to make a difference.

TEACHER TALK *Insights & Emerging Understanding*

Assessing multiliteracies requires a model that captures both the process and product of many different kinds of learning experiences. Our assessment model provides ways for students to self-assess, reflect on the entire learning engagement from start to finish, and take ownership of their learning process. Today's students have access to an overwhelming amount of information and an abundance of resources that are available with the click of a mouse. But they need to be critical consumers of knowledge, able to explore the author's/designer's intent, perspectives, and audiences. They need to look at the implications of their learning and explore ways to use their knowledge to make a difference for themselves and others. Most of all, students must recognize how their learning experience affects their own identities and moves them toward being socially responsible, critically literate citizens in a global world.

Students today must also make decisions about the best multimodal tools to use for interpreting and sharing their learning. Traditional assignments and projects such as essays, reports, and posters can be expanded to include e-books, movies, slideshows, and podcasts. Assessment tools must provide ways to capture the richly layered expressions of understanding as students design Web sites, post on blogs and wikis, share documents on Google Docs, and produce a wide range of multimedia projects for various audiences both in and outside of school.

Suggestions to Get Started with Our Assessment Model

Phase 1: *Planning*

Begin with a planning document that addresses all six categories: Content, Intent or Purpose, Audience, Composition/Design, Social Action, and Reflection.

() Describe each category, providing examples and questions to discuss with the students.

() Create a time line or checklist to guide the assignment.

() Schedule checkpoints and conferences with students.

() Design mini-lessons to support student understanding of project content or assessment categories. For example:

- Research skills
- Editing
- Design principles

Phase 2: *Involvement*

() Create a plan for gathering anecdotal data.

- Notes
- Checklists
- Portfolios
- Video or audio data
- Student artifacts

() Encourage and explore multiple perspectives.

Phase 3: *Evaluation of Learning*

() Students reflect on each category in the planning document as they address the final product.

- This can be a written narrative.
- Point values can be assigned to categories.
- Participation can be an added category.
- Encourage all comments, suggestions, and questions.

Favorite Books Used in Student Inquiry Projects About Endangered Animals

(See Appendix U for more text suggestions.)

Almost Gone: The World's Rarest Animals by S. Jenkins

The Bald Eagle—Endangered No More by M. Priebe

The Best Book of Endangered and Extinct Animals by C. Gunzi

Can We Save Them? Endangered Species of North America by D. Dobson and J. Needham

Eaglet's World by E. Minshull

Eyewitness: Endangered Animals by B. Hoare

Returning Wildlife: The Bald Eagle by J. Becker

Soaring with the Wind: The Bald Eagle by G. Gibbons

Chapter 5

Book Clubs and the Biography Project: Differentiation Through Critical Engagements

Jenny passionately reads her journal connection with members of her book club group: "I love the way Coretta kept Dr. King's dream alive. It was also great how she made a center for nonviolence. I wish she were still alive today so I could meet such a remarkable lady. She is a role model. I have a good connection to this book."

Around the room at various tables, Mary's third graders are engaged in other book club discussions about Roberto Clemente, Harry Houdini, and Eugenie Clark (see Figure 5.1 for the list of books used with this unit on biographies). At first glance, these book groups seem like any other literature discussions. The students are sharing connections, asking questions, discussing characters, making predictions, and engaging in the practices that support good conversations about literature. But listening carefully, we notice significant differences between a typical book discussion and the way Mary's students are talking about their books.

Because they are used to asking and discussing *critical questions* and using the Language of Multiliteracies, they easily transfer this process into their book discussions. When in doubt, they know they can refer to

Figure 5.1

BIOGRAPHY BOOK CLUB SELECTIONS

- *Dare to Dream: Coretta Scott King and the Civil Rights Movement* by Angela Shelf Medearis
- *Read It to Believe It! Houdini's Last Trick* by Elizabeth A. Hass
- *Shark Lady: True Adventures of Eugenie Clark* by Ann McGovern
- *We'll Never Forget You, Roberto Clemente* by Trudie Engel

classroom anchor charts that include the key vocabulary and reminders to consider various perspectives.

As we walk around the room we hear students exploring multiple points of view:

"Well, if the mom were telling the story . . ."
"Maybe the author wants us to consider . . . , but I think . . ."

We also hear students using vocabulary from multiliteracies to explain their observations:

"Notice how the font changes . . ."
"Look at that 'demand' image . . ."
"We can make a link to this information."
"Red will grab the reader's attention."

The students use laptop computers and iPads to record conversations, search for pictures, make connections, or express ideas. Students who are not in groups are reading selections to prepare for their meetings or working on responses to share with their groups. Using iPads, Ryan's group writes responses to Roberto Clemente's story. In a back corner of the room, Jamie uses crayons and markers to create an elaborate drawing of an action scene from Houdini's biography. Jenny's group is having a heated discussion about Coretta Scott King as a mother, wife, and social activist. D.J.'s group is writing questions and answers for a book they are putting together with information about how to become an ichthyologist based on Eugenie Clark's experiences. There is a busy buzz in the room as Mary circulates among the groups, joining in conversations, asking probing questions, modeling her thinking, and busily taking notes about student comments and instructional needs that she can turn into mini-lessons.

🌍 The Past Informs the Future

The biography project with third graders is similar to one we developed in Mary's first-grade classroom some years ago. Our focus then—and now—was to help students connect their own life experiences to what they were reading in school. We knew the importance of developing background knowledge, exploring students' questions around a topic, gathering resources, and responding to students' interests as units were developed. We also recognized the need to challenge stereotypes, examine assumptions, and take some kind of action, although we didn't call it critical literacy then. At that time we were starting to use interest groups as a way to provide students with topics they wanted to learn about, while also teaching skills and strategies required by the district curriculum. In first grade—and now in third grade—the students have shown us the power of interest groups to create a feeling of community and provide a way for natural differentiation to occur.

For example, Amy and Lisa would seem to be unlikely partners for an inquiry about Oprah Winfrey (part of a first-grade biography unit). Amy is an advanced reader and a leader in the classroom. Lisa has many idiosyncrasies and learning issues, never quite fitting in. She seems to live on the fringes, with low self-esteem preventing her from fully participating with the rest of the class. But her burning interest in Winfrey gave her the courage to ask to work with Amy. Because of their common interest, the girls formed a relationship, and Lisa has blossomed through the shared experience.

In our anecdotal observations, we note the girls' fascination with the many ways Winfrey helped others and overcame great obstacles in her life. On their own, the two girls decided to use a talk-show format and dramatize an interview with Winfrey. Amy became the interviewer, and Lisa took the role of Oprah, using their dialogue to share their thoughts about important social issues with the entire class.

Lisa: Oprah had to work really hard to get into television and to become a big star.

Amy: Yes, it was harder for her because she was a woman.

Lisa: Most of the jobs in TV and radio were men's jobs. It seems like you still see more men on TV today.

Amy: That isn't fair! Girls can do as good a job— maybe better. Oprah proved that!

Lisa: And she had to work even harder because she was black, too.

When we started using interest groups in Mary's first-grade classes, we didn't name students' work *critical engagements*. But Amy and Lisa were doing more than just sharing facts about Winfrey. They were exploring social issues and making personal connections. We didn't call the classroom environment a *community of practice*, but Lisa and Amy valued each other's perspectives and participation, working together to create their projects and generate greater understanding through their collaboration.

🌍 The Present

Today there are increased opportunities for students to learn and present information, particularly with the tools of technology and the reach of the Internet. Yet these wonderful resources also present new challenges ranging from online safety considerations to analyzing the reliability of information provided on Web sites. One of the greatest needs is for students to recognize that their learning may be local (in the classroom) but also can have global connections (beyond the classroom). Increasingly diverse classrooms include students with varied life experiences, cultures, and languages, so we must intentionally discuss stereotypes and make students aware of unexamined biases and assumptions. School is a great place to help even our youngest students learn to embrace and celebrate differences. It is also a safe, nurturing environment for students to learn how to make informed choices (about who to work with, books to read, and projects to show their learning) and to become reflective as they self-assess their accomplishments in collaboration with the teacher.

Taking responsibility for their learning and connecting to the classroom community should be very important components of the curriculum. Learning is not just about covering content; it is about becoming a responsible citizen. We believe that curriculum is a metaphor for the kind of people we want our students to be. While there are academic requirements, benchmarks, and standards, we also believe that curriculum represents an organic experience that must support diverse learners and remain open to issues and topics that children care about (Vasquez et al. 2004). Children should have opportunities to explore complex issues concerning race, class, or poverty; consider different points of view; and gain insight through their shared learning experiences as seen in the following example.

Cam: Coretta Scott King was a great lady. She let black children go to
school with white children and helped people understand that what

really matters is how you are on the inside and not how you look on the outside. It wasn't easy for her because people don't listen to a woman—especially a black woman.

Kyle: I agree with Cam. Coretta did so much for our country; she deserves a lot of respect. I look up to Coretta because she made a difference. I didn't know much about her until we started to read her biography. I chose the book because I knew about her husband [Martin Luther King, Jr.].

Adam: Coretta was brave; she helped Martin with the bus boycott—you know the one that Rosa Parks started [referencing the book, *I Am Rosa Parks*].

Jenny: Yes, Coretta Scott King was a great role model, and I would follow her. If I lived in that time as a white girl, I would help Coretta, Martin, and Rosa Parks. I would support them and try to make a difference. I think Coretta was very important. If we did not have amazing people in that time, we would not see some of the people we know today. What if Gaby was not here? [This is in reference to an African-American classmate.] We would not be the class we are now! Coretta knew that was wrong and she made a change!

Victor: I agree with Jenny. Coretta is a great role model for us to follow. She really helped our world with friendship and peace.

Karen (barely audible): I wrote something . . .

Jenny: Wow! Good for you. What did you write?

Karen (a little louder now): Here's what I think Coretta said: "I will keep the dream alive! Even though my husband died. We solved our differences between the blacks and whites. Keep the dream alive!"

Conversations like these demonstrate how even young students are able to recognize and understand complex racial issues and relationships. When encouraged to consider difficult social issues, they can begin to identify and consider marginalization and oppression of minorities from a historical perspective over time. We know students can comprehend and retell a story at high levels of understanding. As the students discuss books, they are not just repeating facts. They are synthesizing, reflecting, relating, expressing their own ideas, and connecting with the content of the story.

Students often make personal connections (text-to-self) with what they are reading and share examples from their lives. What's different here is that Mary's students are also evaluating and considering different perspectives as well as social issues as part of their conversation. For example, Jenny feels strongly that if she were living during the time period in her book, she would have helped the Kings. She states that she would "support them and try to make a difference." Jenny has a growing awareness of racial issues and understands that Coretta Scott King and Martin Luther King's work helped make desegregation possible so students of different races could be together in the same school. She connects this to Gaby in her classroom and gains new respect for and insight into the struggles experienced by many African Americans in our country.

Like many readers, Mary's students make the usual text-to-text connections (Harvey and Goudvis 2007). But they are also thinking more globally, understanding that they can share their thoughts and ideas with students beyond their classroom. For example, Adam easily connects Coretta Scott King's story with the book, *I Am Rosa Parks*, recently read by the class. Victor makes a more global connection (text-to-world) when he identifies the themes of friendship and peace in Coretta Scott King's story. Their talk reveals that in addition to analyzing, evaluating, and synthesizing (on Bloom's taxonomy) and developing higher-order thinking skills, they are also becoming critical readers who can identify and relate to issues of power and social justice.

Differentiating Learning: Content, Process, and Product

The classroom environment that Mary creates is responsive to the needs of her students and the learning groups. Over time she carefully scaffolds her expectations and explains and reviews the various anchor charts while teaching the students how to plan, engage in, and self-assess their learning (assessment model; see Figure 4.2 and Appendix L). In her classroom, differentiation naturally evolves from students' interests, abilities, and talents and the close connections that students build as members of the classroom community.

Mary's role includes careful planning that integrates the required curriculum along with student interests whenever possible (content), establishing clear expectations for student engagement along with explicit procedures (process), and informed monitoring of student progress and outcomes (assessment of process and product). For example, Mary selects a group of books that students can choose for book club reading. The books may be thematic and reflect particular content requirements (such as biographies, personal narratives, and historical fiction), or they may focus on a particular author, or connect to Mary's knowledge of students' interests and reading skills. Mary often previews and bookmarks good

Web sites for student research. Students also know they can access safe search engines like netTrekker and Encyclopaedia Britannica for further investigation and for locating additional materials.

Mary has different groups for different purposes. She has guided groups for specific skill instruction, but interest groups and book clubs are primarily heterogeneous. Students choose their groups based on interest in the topic or group inquiry. Differentiation occurs in the resources that students use, in the tools they choose to work with, and in the products they create to demonstrate knowledge. For example, in book clubs students have learned a variety of ways to respond to their reading. These include written journal responses where students might summarize their reading, share connections and opinions, or ask questions. Students may also respond by creating pictures, story maps, or character sketches.

More recently, these conventional responses have been supplemented by digital components. For example, when Ryan shared a drawing that he did about Roberto Clemente's entrance into the Hall of Fame, he included an actual photo of the event and statistics about Clemente's baseball career found on a Web site. Many of the students prefer to type their responses on the computer, using different fonts and layouts or designs to make their points. Some students will e-mail responses directly to Mary, either from home or while working in the classroom. One group of students even set a schedule of when they would post their responses on their wiki page (Figure 5.2).

Mary also sets up procedures and processes for students to follow as they read their book selections. Students often write journal responses to

Figure 5.2
A book club group creates a schedule for posting from home to their wiki page.

connect with their reading and share with their group. They may identify vocabulary words for further study, questions to share and discuss with the group, predictions about further reading, and reflections about their own learning including how well (or not) the group participated together with suggestions for improvement. Mary continuously monitors participation and looks for ways to scaffold individual students' learning. If a student needs additional support, she will sometimes assign a more capable peer as a partner or find time to work with a student one-on-one or in a small group. At times she has the help of support staff including the English language learner (ELL) teacher, who works with a small group of students in Mary's classroom two times a week, or the learning disabilities specialist, who is a resource teacher for a few of Mary's students.

Anecdotal notes provide ongoing information about student participation and learning needs. During whole-class debriefing after book club, Mary might share some of her observations and ask the students the same critical questions they are learning to ask about the books they are reading and discussing. "So how did your book club meeting go today? What did you notice about the group participation? Did everyone get a chance to talk? Whose voices were heard the most? Who didn't say anything? Why is that? What can you do differently next time? Did you consider different perspectives or points of view?"

Mary also shares her individual observations with students as she encourages them to self-evaluate their learning. She might suggest that Andy read some other material about Houdini and bring it to the group. Or she might encourage Naomi to pay attention to the way an author uses adjectives to make a character come alive for the reader. During a read-aloud/think-aloud, Mary might note the way an author positions the reader to consider particular issues or perspectives. For example, when reading Roberto Clemente's story, Mary guided the group to discuss why Clemente was described as a humanitarian and what that word truly means. She discussed gender inequities with the Shark Lady group by wondering aloud about Eugenie Clark's decision to pursue a career as an ichthyologist although many people suggested that she learn to type and become a secretary to an ichthyologist. As a participant in book club discussions, Mary is always teaching informally. At the same time she also jots down anecdotal notes that will inform future guided instruction, mini-lessons, and grouping possibilities.

When designing projects to share their learning, students will often come up with ideas that are imaginative, interesting, and appropriate. Many of these ideas incorporate technology, so Mary often consults the technology teacher or the librarian about how to add music to a podcast, for example. Sometimes she sends small groups of students to the computer lab for instruction on a skill, and they, in turn, teach the other classmates and Mary about it. A favorite new way of representing understanding is by creating student-written e-books on the iPad. Students love to see their work published and enjoy reading each other's stories (see Figure 5.3).

Figure 5.3

JESSIE'S E-BOOK ON CORETTA SCOTT KING

Coretta Scott King

Was She Really Amazing?
Coretta Scott King is someone we will always remember! She had courage and she was willing to risk her life to help others. African Americans needed her and she came at the right time. How did she become the person that she was?

Coretta's Early Life
Coretta Scott King was born on April 27, 1927 in Marion, Alabama. Her mother's name was Bernice McMurray and her father's name was Obadiah (everyone called him Obie.) Coretta had older and younger siblings who all helped her in different ways. Once when Coretta's house burnt down she found something positive to think about! Coretta had a great childhood because her parents wanted her to have the best things she could and they taught her that she was as good as any white child. When Coretta got older she still felt that way. She wanted to make a change in the way "colored" people were treated!

The class wiki also provides opportunities for students to create their own pages that may include links to primary source materials or to multimedia presentations they have created. Each book club has a home page with links to individual and group contributions (see Figure 5.4). Students can design projects and presentations that match their interests, experiences, and abilities, providing natural opportunities for differentiation. Projects have included Adam's slideshow about Houdini, with a link to a magic trick he performed; Jenny's written report with photos and inspirational quotes from Coretta Scott King found through an Internet search; and a student-made video clip of a scene from Roberto Clemente's life story acted out by book-club members. Music from GarageBand was used in Jackie's and Daniel's project that expresses their understanding of Eugenie Clark's excitement and bravery when diving with sharks. The

Figure 5.4

ROBERTO CLEMENTE GROUP'S WIKI DISCUSSION PAGE

What a great baseball player he was!
Welcome to this page about Roberto Clemente -
the great baseball player from Puerto Rico!

This page was created by: Laurie, Katie, Justin, Adam, Ryan

<-Check out this awesome picture of Roberto Clemente.

<-Check out this cool picture of Roberto Clemente.

<-Roberto had a lot of successes! Click on the link if you want to see a cool picture of one of his awards!!!

<-Check out this writing I wrote about Roberto Clemente.

A chat:

4-14-11 Justin
I really like how Roberto is so determined. He gets so many hits in his games even though once his manager told him not to swing at every ball.

4-17-11 Laurie
I agree with Justin. Roberto was very determined. But he was also a very kind and loving person.

4-18-11 Dr. Shorey
I agree. Roberto was both a talented ball player, and a humanitarian. Do you know what that means?

range of multimodal tools and available resources supports the interests and skills of all students.

We use differentiation strategies to help students learn about content, recognize their thinking process, and evaluate their learning outcomes or products. A lot of preparation goes into the structure, scaffolding, and ultimate instruction reflected in the anchor charts around the classroom and the experiences we have written about. It is also important to consider how these components all work together to support learning that is differentiated and student focused.

Student-Focused Differentiation

Jenny is a student who consistently seeks ways to enrich and extend her everyday work. Mary expects Jenny to take risks and challenge herself. But she expects this of all students, not just the ones who have access to digital tools and perform at high levels. Haley is in the same book club as Jenny, and in a discussion group Haley shares a drawing that she did in response to her reading about Coretta Scott King. The group members are impressed with Haley's effort and affirm her work with comments such as, "Haley, you are a good artist." "I can see how hard it was for Coretta when people treated her bad . . . just look at her face." Haley blushes, feeling validated as the sharing continues. When it is Jenny's turn to share, she shows her peers the Coretta Scott King project she developed, which includes actual photos of Coretta. Haley quickly responds, "Wow, Jenny, how did you get those photos? They are amazing. Can you help me do that?" Jenny immediately answers, "Sure," and the next day Haley and Jenny are diligently working together on a classroom computer as Jenny shows Haley how to find and embed photos into a piece of writing.

When the biography book clubs end, Mary asks the students to form new groups with classmates from each of the four groups. Their assignment is to discuss the similarities and differences of the people they read about in their biographies. Listening in, we hear amazing connections in the students' conversations:

"Both Roberto Clemente and Coretta Scott King were treated poorly because they were African Americans and they were discriminated against."

"Houdini was brave, and so was Coretta."

Students were able to compare and contrast, looking beyond simple facts and recall to a richer analysis of how their important person impacted the lives of others. They discussed the qualities that made these people famous and looked for ways they could use the person as a role model, emulating the qualities that made a difference. Many of these literacy experiences such as book clubs, interest groups, read-alouds, and writing workshop are familiar to all teachers. But looking at these practices with a critical lens expands differentiation in ways that support social action and reflection.

Adding a Critical Dimension to Differentiation

We all know that any group of learners has a wide variety of needs, and it is important to know our students' strengths, weaknesses, interests, and cultural backgrounds in order to provide instruction that presents a range of experiences that reinforce and expand meaningful learning. We also have a responsibility to provide both support and enrichment opportunities for all learners. This is especially important given the many new digital tools that are available and the increasing numbers of students with special needs and language and learning differences. Differentiated instruction typically involves designing instructional content, learning processes, and outcomes or products to meet the needs of diverse students. Teachers generally achieve this by assessing prior knowledge, administering pre/post tests to determine levels and learning needs, offering choices of assignments or topics to study, and providing a range of resources and activities to challenge all students. Although these practices are usually effective, when a critical dimension is added to differentiation, an important shift occurs. The classroom community becomes more accepting of difference, and when everyone (teacher and students) recognizes and acknowledges the many talents, backgrounds, and strengths of all the members, learning problems and language issues are minimized, and opportunities for differentiation naturally occur. What really matters is the recognition that every student is special and has a particular interest or expertise. When this is part of the classroom culture, students become technology experts, artists, writers, readers, scientists, mathematicians, dancers, singers, or actors. Students have the option of working with others who complement or supplement their talents or needs. They are able to choose projects and then have opportunities to work with a heterogeneous group of students who form naturally around a common interest.

Recognizing everyone's special strengths provides status and acceptance for all the students, and this contributes to the formation of a positive classroom community as a whole. It is expected that students will work together and have shared learning experiences. This is in contrast to an overreliance on teacher-formed groups that rarely change or the stigma of being in a particular level or tier. Student choices, shared inquiries, and classroom collaboration don't replace guided practice for students who have specific instructional needs. However, they provide an opportunity for all students to work together regardless of their language, reading level, talents, interests, or learning issues. Caring about each other takes on more importance and the words *learner* and *teacher* apply to everyone in the classroom. It's a shift that first grader Christine identifies in a conversation with a classmate when she says, "We have a lot of learners in our room. And Dr. Shorey, you're a learner too." Raquel adds, "Yes, you go to college . . . you're a student like us." But then Christine jumps in, interrupting, "No, Raquel, that's not what I mean. She teaches us things, but we teach her things, too!"

We believe the foundation for critical differentiation starts in a critical community of practice where many ways of participation are valued (see Figure 5.5 and Appendix Q).

Figure 5.5

CRITICAL COMMUNITIES OF PRACTICE

( ) A *critical community of practice* emphasizes:
- "Who are we?"
  - We honor multiliteracies, prior experiences, cultures, and interests.
  - We respect all perspectives.
- "What are we interested in?"
  - We study the required content.
  - We focus on shared questions/inquiries.
  - We are responsive to individuals and the group.
  - We care about and support each other.

( ) Participation is the expectation.
- All forms of participation are valued.
- Collaboration is encouraged.
- The teacher is the lead learner.
- Students also share leadership or expert roles.

( ) Ownership in the learning process is shared.
- Students are advocates for their own and each other's needs.
  - Opportunities for support and enrichment are available.
  - Choices are part of all learning engagements.
  - Shared goal setting and reflective, responsive instruction is the norm.

An important difference in a critical community of practice is shared responsibility for meeting individual and group needs, and working together to accomplish the goals of the community, which often lead to some kind of social action.

Students feel validated and believe that, "Yes, I can do this." There is a shift in roles so that directing learning isn't the sole responsibility of the teacher. Instead, it is shared with the students, who begin to understand the need to make good choices and challenge themselves to do more than expected. Creativity and independence are nurtured, and students are encouraged to always do their "personal best" (see Figures 5.6 and 5.7).

Figure 5.6
First graders work together on a display of healthy foods.

Figure 5.7
Nidhi and Nikita share their common heritage.

Participation and collaboration become essential for researching information, producing outcomes (work), and demonstrating learning. When students understand that their contributions are valued and encouraged, whether they have beginning skills or higher-level abilities, everyone can participate together on an equal basis. Learning opportunities become differentiated and are constantly changing, regardless of the content, process, or product.

When we add a critical lens to differentiation, our anchor charts, models for instruction, and the assessment model become resources that help support an expanded curriculum and inquiry group learning. For example, students refer to the critical questions all the time. Regardless of the subject or content, they know to ask about voice, perspective, and social action. Even the traditional "W-H" questions are redesigned and have a critical focus. They help students to think more about social justice, point of view, and author's intent (see Figure 5.8).

Mary's students are partners with her in setting goals, evaluating their growth over time, and celebrating their accomplishments. Our assessment model becomes a guide and planning tool to support differentiation and make student learning visible for assessing both process and products (see Figure 4.2 and Appendix L). It helps teachers scaffold instruction and directs them toward needed resources. More important, it provides a concrete way for students to self-assess their learning. By the time students finish working through the planning document and move through the sections of the assessment model, they are able to self-assess their product, analyze their process, and identify their learning. In addition to the assessment model, the group work and talk helps students see what they have accomplished, identify what they still need to do, and figure out how to do it.

Figure 5.8

RESOURCES THAT SUPPORT CRITICAL DIFFERENTIATION

Critical Questions (Fig. 1.2 and Appendix A)
Redesigned W-H Questions (Fig. 2.14 and Appendix F)
Language of Multiliteracies Chart (Fig. 3.6 and Appendix G)
Assessment Model (Fig. 4.2 and Appendix L)
  - a guide for planning and organizing
  - a tool for assessing ongoing learning
Expanded Curriculum Model (Fig. 2.5 and Appendix E)
  - provides opportunities for critical connections and authentic engagements
  - provides opportunities for using many different multimodal tools
  - supports skill development for collaboration, problem solving, creativity, and communication

One of the main tenets of differentiation is customizing resources and instruction to meet the needs of each learner. Digital tools are becoming more available to schools through grants and other funding opportunities. As more and more students gain access to digital resources, teachers must be careful not to misuse them. Access to technology is not enough. If these modern tools are not used in meaningful ways, they become just another "worksheet" or drill/skill experience for the students. We must use technology to support learning and provide broader possibilities for information and answers to questions to accomplish learning objectives. Learning is not just about using tools—it's about using tools for expanded thinking and deeper insight. For example, when Mary's students use an iPad to create a podcast, they do so only after they have prepared scripts that ask critical questions of information found on the Internet. An Internet search and report on a subject shows ways that students are exploring and considering various perspectives. And when students design a slideshow, they not only present information, but also show their learning in ways that may suggest social action.

Mary's students know that talk is part of inquiry. When visitors stop by the classroom, they notice a lot of conversation going on. We know this is purposeful talk and rarely worry about students being "off-task." We caution them to be "quietly enthusiastic," but their passion for a subject or project often bubbles over into a collective classroom buzz that excites all of us and provides evidence of important learning. We would worry if the room was too quiet. Book club talk is a vivid example of how excited the children become when working together on subjects they care about. Listening in, we can hear so many connections made between these famous people and the students' own lives.

Ethan: Harry Houdini was very brave, especially when he did the escape trick with handcuffs.

Jenny: How did he do that?

Ethan: He jumped off a New York bridge handcuffed, in a straitjacket, upside down, and he escaped!

Jenny: Wow! Coretta Scott King was brave, too—in a different way. She and Martin, her husband—you know Martin Luther King—they did lots of brave things like the bus boycott.

Laurie: I remember that. My person is Roberto Clemente, and he was brave, too. He didn't even know English. He couldn't play in the major leagues at first because he was black, sort of—I mean they had too many black players already. It wasn't fair, but he didn't give up.

Allen: Well, my person, Eugenie Clark, she was brave. She swam with sharks!

Mary: Great connections. They were all brave—I heard something else in your talk, too. They all didn't give up—can you think of a word that describes that quality?

Allen: Determined?

We have spent a lot of time analyzing how we support students' learning to ask questions and make connections that help them see the "bigger picture"—to move beyond simply recalling facts, retelling, and making superficial connections. Mary admits that in the descriptions of her classroom, she tends to make everything sound like it just magically happens. In reality it takes a lot of time and practice. Each group of students presents a unique profile, individual needs, challenges, and strengths. Asking critical questions and exploring perspectives is a strand that has connected all of Mary's instruction across all the subject areas. Book clubs and interest groups are powerful strategies for developing critical communities of practice, sharing a common language, asking critical questions, and expanding curriculum in authentic ways.

Parents: An Important Part of the Community

At the end of the school year, Mary and Penny often invite a small group of parents to come and share their thoughts about their children's learning throughout the year (see Figure 5.9). Jenny's mom starts the conversation: "There is something different about this classroom. In fact, I saw it when Jenny was in Mary's first-grade classroom, and I see it again now that she

Figure 5.9
Parents share their perspectives.

is in Mary's third-grade class. The kids really have a sense of ownership. For example, when Jenny asks a question or shares a comment, Mary answers, 'That's a really interesting question or idea. Why don't you see if you can find the answer to that,' and the kids go off and research their own questions. Learning seems very purposeful. Students feel that they can pursue their own interests, and they are always excited and motivated about what they are doing."

Another parent adds, "It is empowering, but don't you think it's just kids today—that they are more sophisticated?"

He is interrupted by a mother who adamantly replies, "I think I can address that. Yes, kids may be more sophisticated, but this classroom is different. When I compare it with my other children's experiences—and they had good experiences—there are differences. One is Andy's involvement. He is so interested in his learning. Right now he's reading about Houdini, and he networks with friends in this class. It's not unusual for him to call up a classmate and talk about his reading. They've looked Houdini up on the Internet and want to do a shared report and a chat on the wiki."

Jackie's mom nods in agreement, "The kids are really connecting because of what they are doing. It may be a book that they are reading or a project they are doing."

Andy's mom continues, "I think it's because they get to *choose* what they are reading or learning. Andy said that he picked Roberto Clemente for his biography. But because he got to have two favorite choices, he knew that he would get one of them. He's happy with Houdini and knows he can read about Clemente later on. That is huge."

"I agree," another parent adds. "My daughter is very quiet, and when she is in a group, she is so excited to do her part, to share. The kids really do work together."

Parent comments always inform and support our teaching and research. Throughout this discussion, parents recognize the many ways the class works together. This is important to us because the children's social networking is a common pattern in Mary's classroom. We want the parents to notice how students participate in conversations about the books they are reading or the content they are learning. We are glad that parents see the importance of choice and understand how motivating it is when students have ownership of their learning.

Like so many teachers, Mary has a classroom made up of students who have a variety of learning needs. There are students like Jenny who have a lot of parental support and access to digital tools at home. There are students like Jared who only get to use computers at school. ELL students like

Shariq may have the tools, but need support communicating and expressing ideas. And there are students like Haley who don't have a lot of home support or access to computers. Regardless of access, need, or competency, Mary has clear goals and expectations for participation from each of her students.

The use of a class blog and wiki has helped Mary keep the parents informed about her curriculum, and parents are becoming more informed and knowledgeable about ways that Mary expands units of study to incorporate group inquiries, provides opportunities for wide reading, and extends discussion around topics with social relevance.

During a parent meeting, Penny asks, "How do you feel about your children's sense of empowerment to take some action, to make a difference?" Jack's dad replies, "Well, what I have seen is Jack's enthusiasm about the things he is learning. He comes home and almost always feels compelled to educate the rest of the family about some of the life lessons he is learning here. He'll talk about sophisticated issues and inform us all that we have to do something. For example, the recent earthquake and tsunamis in Japan have captured his interest. Jack has carefully explained to us that it is our responsibility to help the victims. He's very excited about 'Bracelets for Japan' and he genuinely wants to make a difference."

Mary agrees, "I am always challenging the students to look at the subjects we are learning about, events in the media, any issues we have here in class or on the playground. I encourage students to ask critical questions [pointing to her anchor chart hanging on the wall]. Questions like, 'Whose interests are being served?' or 'What is another way to look at this?' help students to respect other perspectives, to listen more thoughtfully, and to understand. My hope is that as students engage in thoughtful, critical engagements, this will translate to the idea that we should share our learning and do something with it whenever we can."

We have found parents to be our strongest allies and supporters if they are informed about what is happening in the classroom and understand the purpose for some of the units and curricular content. At a parent meeting early in the school year, Mary explains the importance of helping children critique all the media messages, using the critical questions to analyze Web sites, advertisements, and visual signs and symbols. We share our Language of Multiliteracies chart (see Figure 3.6 and Appendix G) and discuss the vocabulary unique to visual, digital, and print literacies in today's world. For example, we talk about how visual literacy used to be the domain of the art class and its vocabulary included words like *sketch, paint,* and *draw.* But today, visual forms include design expressions and vocabulary influenced by digital media, such as *fonts*, *graphics*, and *multimodal designs*. We point out that vocabulary of critique helps students understand that they can use language to bring about change, and that there are powerful words such as *love, care,* or *freedom* that move us to take social action.

The parents linger after their meeting with us, obviously enjoying sharing and telling stories about their children's learning in Mary's room. "For Laurie, it's posting on the wiki that is motivational," one mother explains. "I have really seen her writing improve. She loves the idea that her grandparents in Florida can read her work. And she enjoys the comments that her classmates post about her writing."

Another mother picks up the thread. "Yes, I can't believe the ways that Katie is using technology. She's even teaching her fifth-grade brother a few things."

"When I come in here for learning conferences, students almost always bring a laptop and share some writing or project they are working on," adds another mom. "That is different than it was just two years ago when my son was in first grade."

Karen's mom shares a strong insight about the students' learning. "I was thinking that Dr. Shorey was assigning so much homework. Karen spends an inordinate amount of time on her reading, and she is always asking to use the computer. But then I found out Karen is actually creating the work for herself because she wants to do it. For her biography project, she has been looking for photos of Coretta Scott King. She is finding inspirational quotes to share and creating a response to her reading that is really quite unbelievable. I am really impressed with her motivation and passion. She wants to share her response with her book club group, and she wants it to be just right!"

"I agree," adds Caleb's mom, "Caleb has started a family book club modeled after the ones you do in class. I'm afraid that my husband doesn't always keep up, and Caleb is quite hard on him. He reminds Dave that it is his responsibility, and we need to have shared conversations! It's really kind of fun."

And then, Jenny's mom shares a powerful example of how Jenny applied her learning about community, government, and action when she took it upon herself to enter a writing contest sponsored by the village of Buffalo Grove (Illinois) Chamber of Commerce titled, "Why I love Buffalo Grove." Jenny's contest entry follows:

> *Buffalo Grove is the most exciting community you could ever live in! We are united to our neighbors. Our community helps and cares for*

one another. We are the people who will really make a difference! We start here in Buffalo Grove by donating and volunteering. We donate money to the people and organizations that need the money. I have volunteered in Buffalo Grove by going to a food pantry and adopting families through the township. I love helping and watching our community grow!

Buffalo Grove has lots of beauty. We have fun experiencing the four seasons—winter, spring, summer, and fall. In Winter, we see the beauty of the white snow. In Spring, we see the pretty flowers. In Summer, we dive deep in the pool and splash each other. In Fall, we see the colorful leaves. I love seeing the four seasons because they each have their own beauty. Sometimes it makes Buffalo Grove stand out!

Buffalo Grove has something to make everyone happy! Our community has different places to go. We have parks, pools, sport places (baseball diamonds), gardens, places to eat, shopping malls, banks, movie theaters and more. We appreciate what we have because we have a lot. I am proud to say we have a clean community. Not everyone could say that. I think Buffalo Grove has a lot of good places to go and visit. We take care of these places. I hope we have lots of places like this for a long time.

Buffalo Grove has great leaders! Our representatives are wonderful. They listen to our thoughts and ideas and try to make Buffalo Grove a better place for everyone. Most of them make sure our taxes are not too high. I think our leaders make good choices! Some places in the world don't have good leaders like we do!

Buffalo Grove is full of great people who help us get through tough times! I hope Buffalo Grove can always be this way. We should always be united. I don't think anyone can change our helping and caring ways! When we put it all together we make a great community!

We are impressed with Jenny's writing but not really surprised that she won the contest. From a beginning writer in Mary's first-grade classroom to the more accomplished writer that she is today, Jenny demonstrates that she intuitively understands the power in language and can use her writing to convey messages or make a difference. We are also pleased to see that lessons learned in Mary's classroom about the importance of community and caring about each other and the world have helped give her confidence to act on her beliefs.

We chuckled about the part where she talked about leaders and taxes. We could see evidence of her understandings from our government unit.

But more than that, we could see how the language and words she used showed an awareness of her audience. When we mentioned this, her mom said that when she asked Jenny why she wrote that part, Jenny replied, "Well, I wrote that in case the village leaders were reading my piece!"—very savvy for a third grader. A few weeks later, when the winners of the contest were announced, the whole class celebrated Jenny's accomplishment, and we underscored how as a citizen of Buffalo Grove, Jenny was able to make her young voice heard!

Jenny is a strong example of an empowered learner. She is a collaborator, a problem solver, and a creative communicator. In this written piece and in her classroom participation, she demonstrates the ability to use her learning to bring about change. Using our assessment model to analyze Jenny's written piece, we can see that her intention is clear and focused, she puts forth an informed opinion, and she has an awareness of audience, evident in the words she uses and ways she conveys meaning. When we asked Jenny why she entered this contest, she replied, "You know, Dr. Shorey, we learned about being good citizens. I grew up here and I want to make my voice heard." Jenny understands the concept of social action and is taking beginning steps. As a writer, she also understands the value of reflection and wrote a follow-up essay about her excitement at winning the contest and what it meant to her (see Figure 5.10).

Figure 5.10
Jenny's Reflection

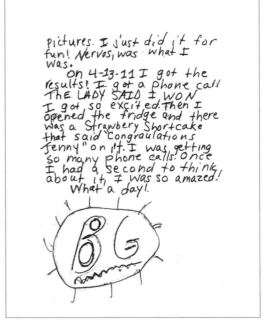

TEACHER TALK   *Insights & Emerging Understandings*

At evaluation time, Mary's principal said to her, "Mary, I believe that you differentiate instruction better than anyone I have observed." Mary smiled and replied, "Thank you for the compliment, but I hope you see it is the classroom environment that I have set up even more than what I'm teaching. It's the purposeful building of a community of practice. It's helping my students learn to respect and acknowledge everyone's contributions to the group. It's making sure that we are careful not to privilege our own perspective and are willing to explore multiple perspectives as we learn together. I'm lucky to have so many available tools and resources for my students to use, and I want to be sure students remember that in our classroom we have twenty-three teachers—including me. I'm not the only expert in the group—we have many experts. We learn from each other, and we learn together."

Mary has always looked for ways to design a classroom environment that supports differentiation. The tools and resources of the twenty-first century support her in this process. But there is a significant difference today. As we've discovered throughout our research, this difference is engaging a critical perspective and looking for authentic connections, as discussed in Chapter 1 when students became involved in Grandma Ruth's plight or in Chapter 2 when students began to understand the marginalization and inequities that occurred for victims of Hurricane Katrina. When students can see relevance in their learning and make connections with everyday issues like the importance of "going green" or a focus on wellness including Michelle Obama's goal of fighting childhood obesity, students feel empowered to try to make a difference, even if it's just a shift in attitude or greater awareness of a need.

Redesigning curriculum and instruction involves planning for critical connections and seeking authentic engagements (Figure 2.5 and Appendix E). It means looking at what we already do with a critical lens. For example, when students begin a unit of study, read a new book, or start a project, "best practice" strategies include tapping into prior knowledge or building schema for understanding. When an inquiry perspective is adopted and critical questions are asked, students are challenged not only to acquire knowledge, but also to think at higher levels as they synthesize, create, and evaluate (Bloom 1956). As students continue the learning experience, they are expanding their awareness of content and working toward greater self-understanding. A natural by-product of this learning cycle is critical differentiation. Students can pursue their own interests both within and outside the constraints of curriculum requirements. As they gain skills with multimodal tools, they develop creative and analytical abilities that enrich and extend basic skills and expand literacy practices beyond just reading print.

Critical differentiation is supported by:

() Establishing clear goals and guidelines for assignments (Appendix L)

() Developing and using anchor charts (critical questions, redesigned W-H questions, Language of Multiliteracies [Appendixes A, F, and G])

() Providing a wide variety of multimodal tools and resources for acquiring information and expressing learning

() Offering students choice of books, projects, classmates, tools, materials, and multimodal ways to show their learning

() Creating opportunities for students to work both individually and collaboratively

() Celebrating all contributions, talents, and areas of expertise

Favorite Books Used for Student Biography Projects
(See Appendix R for more text suggestions.)

Dare to Dream: Coretta Scott King and the Civil Rights Movement by A. S. Medearis

Read It to Believe It! Houdini's Last Trick by E. A. Hass

Shark Lady: True Adventures of Eugenie Clark by A. McGovern

We'll Never Forget You, Roberto Clemente by T. Engel

Chapter 6

Transformations:
Visions for the Future

"It can't be the end of the year already. I've still got so much to write about," exclaims Sanketh, clutching a favorite book about his native India to his chest.

Ari follows his lead, "Yep, the Environmental Group is just finishing the recycling posters to put up around the school."

Jessie adds, "I hope we can continue our book club discussions over the summer, if the wiki works. Blake and Jackie want to read with me, and we can keep our discussion going with the wiki."

The end of the school year is always bittersweet for us. We are excited about the students' enthusiasm for inquiry and the depth of understanding that occurred through the year. And yet, like the children, we know there is still so much more to do and share. The best learning tends to happen after a unit of study, when new questions emerge from our shared experiences.

Each year, we experience the closeness of our classroom community, which includes children and their parents and families. Over the past few years, our students have taken to technology with ease, teaching us ways to use it more authentically and seamlessly. Many of them continue learning after school, on the weekends, and well into the summer, thanks to the availability of technology and platforms for collaboration (wikis, blogs, Google Docs, etc.). Their excitement and motivation to learn reaffirms our belief that all children are curious and come to school eager to explore new ideas.

Our work has also shown that young children can think deeply and make connections to the world beyond the classroom. Building a caring community of practice in the classroom sets the stage for students to take learning risks and gain confidence in their ability to think and work collaboratively with others. Learning to ask critical questions from the start and exploring socially relevant and authentic curriculum can result in transformative learning. Each year we have seen how passionate and motivated they become when they are given opportunities to investigate topics of personal interest or explore important events beyond the classroom.

We know the students leave Mary's classroom with an understanding of social issues and the desire to make a difference, take a stand, or at least critique a text. We also believe they have a stronger sense of themselves as capable, successful students who know how to solve problems and evaluate their learning based on collaborative experiences with peers and shared assessment opportunities with the teacher. But we have always wondered how a critical literacy curriculum in the early grades shapes children and affects their identities as they progress through school. So we decided to investigate. We talked with teachers who received Mary's students in the following years. We wanted to see if they noticed any difference in how her former students responded to questions, exhibited leadership, or demonstrated confidence in using technology and pursuing subjects through inquiry projects. We also talked with school administrators to see what they noticed about her students. Additionally, we invited groups of parents to discuss their children's learning. Each of these groups had a lot to say, and their comments validated and challenged our thinking.

Of course, we had to ask the students too. We invited Mary's present and former students to participate in small-group discussions. We hoped that as they shared their memories of significant experiences in her classroom, we would be able to see if their involvement with social justice and critical literacy had a lasting impact on their identity throughout the elementary grades. Results from these meetings helped us understand the complexities of teaching in the twenty-first century and gave us greater insight into how much the children truly enjoy learning about their world.

Our first group was an after-school session with some students from Mary's previous first-grade classes. Most of the students were teenagers now, but they were still excited and happy to be back in Mary's classroom. We noticed that members of the Hurricane Group and Grandma Ruth Group naturally gravitated to their former seats around the table. Soon the conversation sounded like old folks reminiscing about their youth. Here are some snippets of conversation we recorded:

Tori: Remember Grandma Ruth?

Karen: Sure! Her house was an "eyesore"! Wasn't it the government that wanted to take her property?

Tori: We wanted to help. Remember, Bryanna wanted her to go on *Extreme Makeover*. I wanted to clean it up.

Karen: Whatever happened to Grandma Ruth?

Tori: Remember in second grade we tried to find out? Do you know, Dr. Shorey?

() () ()

Blake: I'm still fascinated by weather. Every time I hear about a tropical depression or hurricane, I think of the victims in New Orleans and the work we did to support them.

() () ()

Carly: I'm still trying to figure out how to mediate arguments and help kids get along better. Remember when I tried to set up a peace table in third grade? I was a junior counselor at camp in the summer, and this helped me work with the kids more effectively.

These conversations revealed that the students remembered many of the authentic classroom experiences where they worked to solve real problems or take action toward a positive outcome. We heard nothing about lessons they had been taught. What mattered to them was the collaborative work to achieve a common goal, using all of the literacy skills available to them to do their work. Reflecting on their comments and memories of shared experiences led us to new questions about teaching and learning. Like our students, we are continually engaged in a never-ending cycle of inquiry that helps us refine and rethink our instruction and assessment.

 **Inquiry**

Classmates such as Vicky, Bridget, and Christopher shared that being able to ask questions about topics they cared about and then find answers to their inquiries made learning exciting. Christopher's leadership skills emerged in first grade when he organized an interest (inquiry) group about space. Perceiving that he wasn't fully accepted by many of the students, he was reluctant to read aloud or participate in whole-class discussions. However, through his interest in studying space, he found that other children shared his passion. Thirty minutes a day, during interest group time, he would grab his folder of information and the basket of books that Mary had collected and gather his group for reading, discussions, and research related to space exploration. The only official expectation was to examine several different sources of information and present the learning to the class in an engaging, meaningful way.

Third graders Vicky and Bridget used the class wiki to share their learning about nutrition. Because of their interest in the topic, they read menus, food labels, books about the food pyramids, and online resources, all of which supported their development as readers and writers. Their research led to a suggestion that the student council make the school lunch menu more nutritious and balanced.

For these students and many others, the inquiry model helped them pursue their passions and make new friends. Within and across groups, we found that students felt supported by a classroom community that valued their special talents or areas of expertise. Years after leaving Mary's classroom, students still remembered that Sam was the technology expert, Max the math wiz, Emma the dancer, and Taylor the artist. As teachers we recognized that after establishing the expectations, structure, and tools for working in inquiry groups, the most effective strategy had been to move aside and let the students work together. Our assessment model provided a way for them to become independent learners, focusing on what they wanted to know more about and offering guidance for meeting or surpassing what was expected.

Multimodal Tools

In our first year of research, Sam was a struggling reader who would only write when he was able to use a computer. With a keyboard and mouse in hand, his beginning writing revealed developing knowledge of phonemic awareness and emergent phonetic skills. Using a computer motivated Sam to learn beginning print literacy skills in order to write about sports and about his dog. Sam's stories helped him gradually assume status not only as a sports expert, but also as the class technology expert. This also contributed greatly to a more positive self-image.

Like many of the children, Adam discovered new audiences for his writing through the class wiki. He was motivated to write expressively and experiment with digital tools such as PowerPoint, iMovie, and podcasts. Jaimie won the respect of her classmates by expressing herself artistically through collages, watercolors, and graphics. In turn, she also deepened her understanding of complex topics such as the environment, African-American history, and homelessness. Rhia danced her way to understanding, celebrating her Indian culture and sharing performances on YouTube. Elizabeth's passion for music motivated her to learn how to create and add music to her presentations using GarageBand.

Today's students have new opportunities for learning, whether communicating with pen pals around the world, looking at online museum exhibits, or listening to orchestra performances without leaving the classroom. A major challenge for teachers is helping students use these tools wisely and learn how to evaluate information from a critical perspective, remembering that everyone has particular interests or biases. Other challenges include helping students collaborate and use technology to enhance their learning, not just to drill and practice basic skills. However, while acknowledging students' excitement in using technology, we must teach them to use it in meaningful ways for thoughtful inquiry and critique.

Authentic Experiences and Community

Critical incidents such as Hurricane Katrina and social issues such as recycling and wellness provided ways for students to "live" their learning. By asking critical questions and looking at multiple perspectives, students were better able to understand citizens' rights and responsibilities. As first graders, Karen and Tori began to see gender inequities in the stories they read. It wasn't long before they also recognized and challenged these same issues in the games they played on the playground or in the way some teachers called on boys more than girls. As eighth graders, they still remembered much of the learning they experienced in first grade, including books such as *Ruby's Wish* (Bridges 2001), *Piggybook* (Browne 1986), *The Paper Bag Princess* (Munsch 2000), and *Players in Pigtails* (Corey 2003), which had piqued their interest in racism, stereotypes, and women's rights.

Seventh grader Blake was a member of the original Hurricane Group. The self-proclaimed scientist in that group, he still has a passion for meteorology and weather phenomena. He also recalled how he learned in first grade about the marginalization of blacks during the events surrounding

Hurricane Katrina. He discussed ways that other minorities are oppressed and related this learning to his current studies about World War II and the Holocaust.

Fifth grader Collette is still a strong advocate for environmental issues. She proudly showed us a prized possession: a copy of her sequel to *The Lorax* (Seuss 1971) that she wrote in first grade and posted on the class online home page "for the whole world to see." Collette told us how her role in student council has provided a way for her to work on recycling in the lunchroom and also about her plans to start a blog called "Students Go Green."

Lainie, now in third grade, jumped in and mentioned how her first-grade work on wellness inspired an ongoing interest in nutrition. She recalled how her group created an infomercial about the need for healthy eating and exercising, noting that this is the very same issue that First Lady Michelle Obama is involved in today. She plans to see if Mrs. Obama would be interested in the wiki work that her group has created.

The stories and memories these students shared reminded us of the importance of connecting the curriculum to critical incidents and current events. If we want students to care for the earth and for each other, we need to help them learn that caring begins in a democratic classroom community based on mutual respect. Through their shared experiences they learn that they can make a positive impact in their school, in the neighborhood, and in the world beyond.

🌍 Empowerment to Take Social Action

Carly, Jessie, and Sanketh remember learning that their actions can make a difference. Carly, a seventh grader, talked about how she organized the "gently-used book drive" for the victims of Hurricane Katrina in first grade. With her quick smile and enthusiasm, she described other causes she has been involved in, including organizing a "Peace Table" in second grade where students could resolve differences of opinion. "That sounds like fighting with words," Andrew said, responding to Carly's description during our focus group. The students (all ages) nodded as they recalled one of their favorite read-alouds, *Martin's Big Words* (Rappaport 2001). "Exactly," Carly replied, then continued by describing the walk-a-thons that she is doing for Crohn's disease and, more recently, her involvement in promoting breast cancer awareness.

David remembers his frustration in trying to promote a "waste-free" lunch for the first and second graders and then discovering that even when the children had a favorite food for lunch they still threw out large amounts of garbage. Undaunted, he reminded us that it was his inquiry group that persuaded the principal to place a recycling bin in the lunchroom for the first time. Then Jenny, a current third grader, added, "You have to use your learning to make a difference." She told everyone about how she started the Bald Eagle Group in Mary's classroom and the work they have been doing. Jenny described her research and how the class wiki had provided a platform for promoting the need to protect the bald eagle from extinction. She shared links to organizations that welcome student involvement and encouraged others to join her in preserving endangered species.

The students' conversations and stories bring our Multiliteracies Framework to life (see Figure 1.8). They show us how students thrive when they are able to ask questions they care about, engage with real-life issues, and become both critical consumers of information and effective communicators.

Critical literacy resides at the heart of multiliteracies. Students work together to make a difference for others and for themselves. They learn to examine many points of view, analyze texts, and question practices of privilege and injustice. As informed citizens, students care about each other and the world beyond the classroom and take their civic responsibilities very seriously. Our work has shown that this critical stance can have an enduring impact on the identities of young children. We have also learned that the required curriculum can be immeasurably enriched by including a critical dimension. Rather than an addition to the curriculum, this becomes an integral part of everything that takes place in the classroom, leading to stronger readers and writers, thinkers and problem-solvers. The students' voices, together with our reflections, show the positive impact of critical literacy on student learning and reveal many ways we have changed our understanding and thinking about teaching.

Looking Backward and Moving Forward

As teachers we always wonder how all the learning that takes place in our classrooms impacts our students in the years that follow. Listening to our students confirmed that what mattered most to them was their authentic involvement in real-life experiences where they felt they made a difference, or their voices could be heard. Even if their activities remained at the classroom or school level (for example, recycling, or designing an artifact wall

Figure 6.1
Mary with Her
Current Third
Graders

in the hall), the interactive, collaborative engagements made their learning meaningful. We also knew that through these shared experiences, they were learning not only to read and write and to use technology, but also to critique and think from various points of view and to work together respectfully and productively. Reconnecting with our former students helped us realize how much we had changed as teachers, and also challenged us to continue to look for ways to make literacy and learning even more meaningful for today's students.

Mary's Voice

My own transformation began as I learned more about critical literacy during the first year of my collaborative research project with Penny and Linda. Over time I came to understand that critical literacy isn't a program or a formula or a script. It is a mind-set, a reflective lens, and a belief about teaching and learning. A conversation at the end of our first year of research helped to clarify my beginning understanding:

Mary: How would you define critical literacy?
Linda: Critical literacy involves reading texts from a variety of
    perspectives. Texts are never neutral. Authors have agendas, positions,
    messages, and it is the responsibility of the reader to either accept the
    author's position or to resist it. It involves asking questions like whose
    voice is heard and whose is not. Often times we don't even know an
    author is influencing our thinking—reading critically involves

making the invisible message visible.

Penny: Yes, in your classroom that involved developing the language and questions that were important to ask and then making them a regular part of classroom discussions.

Mary: What about the argument that the students are only first graders—I remember in a graduate class one of my colleagues said, "Mary, your job is to teach them to read and write, not to have a democratic classroom."

Linda: But Mary, Vygotsky's work and sociocultural theory shows us that as students develop, they learn through their language and their interaction with others. Of course your students learned to read and write, but your goals went deeper. You were envisioning the kinds of critical readers and thinkers they could be. Vygotsky reminds us that we must always teach with the end in mind—the skills of reading and writing will develop best in a meaningful context.

Penny: In this case, your goal was to help the students learn to question the text, to think about big social issues like gender and homelessness, and through their use of visual and digital experiences they were learning more than traditional print [reading and writing]. They were learning to read and write and, at the same time, they were learning about reading and writing as purposeful and meaningful acts to communicate important ideas.

Mary: Yes, my early journal entries reflect a struggle to balance traditional instruction and critical literacy. They also show that I didn't really understand what critical literacy involved.

Penny: It is a common dilemma for teachers. We all learned a lot this year. We saw that as students learned to read and write and to question, they were empowered through the use of shared language and critical questions. Next year, you will have a stronger vision of what your outcomes could be and begin to teach toward those goals from the start.

Expanding my understanding of literacy to include a critical perspective transformed my teaching. When I think back to that first year, I remember how I continually asked, "How is this good for kids?" My students showed me and taught me to trust the process. In my heart I knew that I wanted to do much more than deliver programs and teach basic skills, but I worried about covering the curriculum. I was a little defensive, too. I prided myself on having a great classroom community—and I did—but what changed was adding that critical dimension, exploring multiple perspectives, examining issues, and taking some kind of action.

Over time, I have learned to live my vision and my beliefs. In both my personal and professional lives, being critically literate means seeing the whole picture, paying attention to relationships, honoring all perspectives, and looking for ways to use learning to make a difference for myself and others. My identity has changed as a result of this understanding, and I model my thinking daily with my students and colleagues. I find myself asking questions like "What is another way to look at this?" or "Who has a different idea?" and I am more tolerant of others who might think differently than I do about something. My former principal, Jane Kier, wrote in my teacher evaluation: "I have observed how a critical literacy perspective has transformed your professional interactions with colleagues. It is exciting to see you share your expertise with your colleagues in a nonjudgmental way. You have earned their respect by listening to their points of view, and showing them how you expand the curriculum, making room for your students to use the basic skills for thinking, questioning, and reaching out to others. The same compassion, care, and respect you give your students, you share today with your colleagues."

As teachers we understand how important multimodal expression is for our students. We must support the many ways that children can sing, dance, and dramatize their way to understanding. In this era of testing and standardization, when analytical left-brain abilities seem to matter most, I believe that artistic, social, and collaborative right-brain abilities must not be forgotten. With new common core standards and a culture of accountability, it is more important than ever to foster creativity and imagination and to incorporate all of the multiliteracies that will help our students negotiate a changing future.

Penny's Voice

As a former reading specialist and resource teacher in Mary's school, I thought I knew a lot about literacy. I have worked with many different kinds of learners and provided answers for many different literacy issues and problems. Yet it was through my research in Mary's classroom that I discovered the power of critical literacy and multimodal learning. I have become so much more aware of all the ways that we "read" and process information. I now see how visual, digital, and print information work together to provide a broader, more complete understanding of the world. I also recognize how essential it is to include a critical literacy perspective throughout the curriculum. This expanded view of literacy sup-

Figure 6.2
Former students
pose with Penny at
a reunion.

ports naturally differentiated reading and writing across content areas and provides students with opportunities to think deeply about topics that matter to them.

Working with Mary showed me how to model collaboration and shared inquiry for our primary students, for the teachers in Mary's school, and for my preservice and reading specialist students at the university. Together we have seen firsthand how young children are able to:

◊ Take responsibility for their own learning
◊ Become partners with the teacher in assessing their learning
◊ Question, critique, deconstruct, and change stereotypical behaviors and practices
◊ Use all the tools available to them to pursue their own inquiries
◊ Teach us all how to use the newest digital equipment
◊ Form learning groups based on interests and shared expertise
◊ Engage in thoughtful discussions about world (and local) events
◊ Recognize the need to take social action and become involved to make a difference
◊ Learn to love reading and writing in many different genres, because it is the way they learn about their world
◊ Use a variety of media to communicate
◊ Feel passionate about a wide range of issues, topics, and ideas

◯ Question and investigate issues
◯ Consider various points of view and perspectives rather than jumping to conclusions
◯ Participate respectfully and positively within the classroom community of practice
◯ Recognize others' expertise and share their own as they work together collaboratively
◯ Self-assess their strengths, needs, and learning

The children have shown and taught us that they are able to work together purposefully and engage fully to accomplish tasks that they perceive are important. They do not mind working hard if it is for the greater good. But like all of us, they don't want to waste their time practicing what they already know. Like students everywhere, they need opportunities and time to discuss, question, choose, or contribute to their own learning in some meaningful way. Our job is to design a structure for students to function independently, with appropriate scaffolding and guidance. We have found that interest groups (inquiry groups) help children practice all the skills they will need in the world beyond the classroom. When they have opportunities to choose an inquiry focus, classmates to work with, appropriate tools to accomplish their tasks, and an evaluation tool to guide their learning, they can work independently in small groups, function within the whole-class structure, and learn to participate fully as a successful member of the classroom community.

A Shared Conversation: For Mary's Daughter, Natalie, in Her First Year of Teaching, and for All Teachers, Everywhere

We are teaching and learning in a time of rapid change. The learning demands of twenty-first-century classrooms require an expansive view of literacy and learning. There are new tools, new ideas and issues for inquiry, and exciting ways to make a difference. When children are engaged in experiences that are meaningful and have opportunities to collaborate, connect, and think together, the classroom community becomes focused on learning and caring about others. Students not only cover the curriculum, they expand it exponentially when we make time to listen to their questions, honor their inquiries, and look carefully at the everyday signs of

Figure 6.3
Natalie and Her
First-Grade
Students

learning that are occurring.

There will be many demands on our teaching time: programs to implement, assessments to administer, and data to gather. Although we've said this many times, it bears repeating. Remember that we are teaching children, not programs. Each child is unique and brings years of life experience to the classroom. Each child has areas of expertise, special interests, unique needs, and can make significant contributions to your classroom. The curriculum is a road map of learning for the school year. While we are expected to follow it, there are many ways to arrive at a destination. Although we often stay on the main highway (required programs, texts, units of study, benchmarks, objectives, standards), we also need to take time to explore the side roads and learn from the scenery, small towns, and country roads along the way. Through interest groups and inquiry projects, we can provide opportunities for the children to learn the required content and extend their thinking beyond what is expected. Their shared experiences will be more meaningful and will provide opportunities for natural differentiation and more lasting learning.

In our classrooms we need to purposefully ask critical questions such as "Whose voice is heard?" "Whose is not?" or "Who is (or is not) benefiting from this?" "Why is this so, and what can we do about it?" As members of a classroom community, we celebrate our differences, knowing that these are what make us special. We laugh, sing, dance, discuss, compose, and dramatize our understanding. We take risks in a supportive environment. We engage in joyful learning, knowing that the joy comes from a feeling of efficacy and belonging.

And as we seek answers across subject and content areas, new questions will inevitably arise, reminding us that the questions are often more important than the answers. We know that teaching for multiliteracies, building a classroom community of practice, and providing critical engagements cannot be prescriptive. We also know the importance of studying our own practice and reflecting on teaching: thinking about what works in the classroom and what engages the children, and letting these insights help us teach the students more effectively.

We want all of you to love teaching as much as we do and to know that your passion for learning is a beacon to guide and inspire the children in your classroom. Living your life as a socially aware and critically literate role model will give your students guidance, support, knowledge, and love that will sustain them. Best of all, the students will be learning how to live and work in a democratic environment, where difference and diversity are honored, where opinions and ideas can be expressed, where all voices can be heard, and where change and new possibilities are the foundation for lasting learning.

We want teachers to open their students' minds to the possibilities of freedom—to have an image of how to make peace, reject racism, help those in trouble, and guard the earth. We want them to ask their students, "What will you do for the world?" and then help them discover possibilities and develop the knowledge to act on those possibilities (Bomer and Bomer 2001). Today's children are tomorrow's future. Treat them with care and teach them well!

Appendixes

Appendix A

CRITICAL QUESTIONS

- Whose voices are heard? Whose voices are absent?

- What does the author/illustrator want the reader to think/understand?

- What is an alternative to the author/illustrator's message?

- How will a critical reading of this text help me change my views or actions in relation to other people?

Appendix B

EXPANDED FOUR RESOURCES MODEL

	Conventional Curriculum	Expanded Critical Curriculum
Code Breaker	• alphabetic principle • sounds in words • spelling • grammar conventions	• learn about a variety of ways to talk and behave that are unique to cultures, situations, and organizations
Meaning-Maker	• vocabulary instruction • strategy instruction (i.e., predicting, inferring, synthesizing) • compose text (written, oral, visual, or digital)	• tap into student's background knowledge, culture, native language, or prior experiences
Text User	• read and write different genres (fiction, nonfiction, poetry)	• explore purposes of texts and multimodal forms of expression, subtle meanings, hidden messages in words, images, Web sites
Text Analyst (Critic)	• examine author's purpose • engage multiple perspectives	• ask critical questions • act on understandings

Adapted from Luke and Freebody 1999

Appendix C

MULTILITERACIES FRAMEWORK

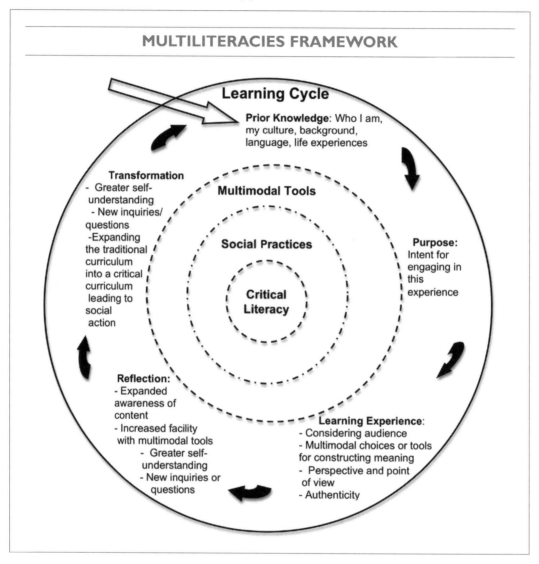

Appendix D

INTEREST GROUP START-UP GUIDE	
Getting Started	Select a topic of interest: • Content area (for example: environment, animal habitats) • Subject choice Form a group (usually 4–6 students). Begin an assessment planning document.
Organizing	Use an organizer (for example: K-W-L or semantic map) to: • Record prior knowledge (K). • Record questions—content & critical questions (W). Gather resources: • Print • Digital • Other
Researching	Explore your topic. Take notes or write down important information (L). Add new questions and continue searching. Build a report, written or digital (wiki). Include pictures, photos, music. Record your sources. • Write down the author, title, and/or URL.
Presenting	Create a sharing plan. Use the assessment planning document to consider the following: • Content • Intent • Audience • Composition/design • Social action • Reflection Construct final product (i.e., slideshow, podcast, video). Share!

Appendix E

EXPANDED CURRICULUM TEMPLATE

_____-Grade Curriculum	Critical Connections	Authentic Engagements

Appendix F

REDESIGNED W-H QUESTIONS

WHO?
- Whose voice is heard? Whose voice is not heard?
- Who is the author (designer/illustrator), and who else could author this piece?
- Who is the audience for this selection, and who else might be interested?

WHAT?
- What perspective is presented? What is another perspective to explore?
- What does the author/illustrator/designer want you to think?
- What are other ways to think about the same idea (topic, event, situation)?

WHERE?
- Where can spaces be opened in the selection for other points of view, ideas, or issues?
- Where did this idea originate, and how could it be more democratic or just?
- Where do authors get ideas?

WHEN?
- When did you notice your thinking changed about the selection?
- When did you engage with this story/design/performance?
- When did you think you understood the selection?

WHY?
- Why did the author choose this genre or these modes for the selection?
- Why do you think this design was selected and for what purpose?
- Why do you think these tools and techniques were used, and what are alternatives?

HOW?
- How can you use this experience to make a difference?
- How do your life experiences affect your understanding and appreciation of the selection?
- How can you use this experience to expand your thinking and to act on your beliefs?

Appendix G

THE LANGUAGE OF MULTILITERACIES: VOCABULARY FOR DESIGN

Critical Literacy

Power in Language	Care
Social Action	Deconstruction
Resistance	Transformation
Perspective	Citizenship

Print Literacy	Visual Literacy	Digital Literacy	Other Literacies
• Fiction • Nonfiction • Writing • Genre • Theme • Author's intent • Comprehension strategies such as predicting, confirming, retelling	• Color and contrast • Size and shape • Line • Patterns and textures • Balance • White space • Position of image (e.g., demand image)	• Font • Link • URL • Podcast • Blog • Wiki	• Movement • Gestures • Music • Drama • Facial expression

Appendix H

VISUAL LITERACY STRATEGIES: MINI-LESSONS

This series of mini-lessons focuses on using picture books to learn more about visual literacy. As each visual design feature is introduced, a classroom chart can be created to highlight the new element.

Color and Contrast

A discussion of color as a design feature usually begins with students discussing what they know or have noticed about the use of color in picture books. This is probably the most common design element for student discussion. Many picture books use color in interesting ways that support, enhance, and create meaning.

    Questions that guide this lesson include:
- What colors does the illustrator use? Why do you think these choices were made?
- Do certain colors depict certain characters or events?
- How does color create a mood or help you understand the story?
    Favorite books:
- *The Color of Home* by Mary Hoffman, Karin Littlewood (illustrator)
- *Heckedy Peg* by Audrey Wood, Don Wood (illustrator)
- *Harlem: A Poem* by Walter Dean Myers

Size and Shape

When introducing these design features, a good book to use is the classic *Round Trip* by Ann Jonas. This book uses the same lines and shapes to depict two different trips—read the book one way, then turn it over and read it again going the other direction. Focusing on pictures rather than words, ask and discuss the following questions:
- What do you notice about these pictures?
- Why do you think the author/illustrator positioned characters, things in certain ways?
- What do you think came first, the pictures or the words?
    Favorite books:
- *Round Trip* by Ann Jonas
- *How Strong Is It?* by Ben Hillman
- *David's Father* by Robert Munsch, Michael Martchenko (illustrator)

Line

A classic book for highlighting line is *Harold and the Purple Crayon*. Every age student delights in this story. When discussing the use of line, expand your focus and conversations to include different kinds of line (i.e., thick, straight, zigzag) and a discussion of ways that the use of line suggests direction, motion, and energy.

    Questions that guide this lesson include:
- How can the use of line help us to see the story?
- Where do the lines direct us?
- Why did the author/illustrator use thick, thin, wavy lines?

(continued)

Appendix H (continued)

Favorite books:
- *Harold and the Purple Crayon* by Crockett Johnson
- *Don't Let the Pigeon Drive the Bus!* by Mo Willems
- *The Gardener* by Sarah Stewart, David Small (illustrator)

Patterns and Texture

An interesting way to discuss the design elements of pattern and texture is to look at the art form of collage. Most students are familiar with this style. A quick "hook" for this mini-lesson is to project an image from any picture book that uses patterns and texture onto a screen. Have students spend time observing the movement or action in the visual image. Sometimes patterns or textures are used as a framing technique; often they are used to instill a realistic effect or to engage the imagination of the reader.

Questions that can stimulate discussion include:
- Is there a consistent pattern or variation?
- How do the pictures create meaning? Is the meaning similar to the words or different?
- Where do you focus first? Why?

Favorite books:
- *Smoky Night* by Eve Bunting, David Diaz (illustrator)
- *A River Ran Wild* by Lynne Cherry
- *The Very Hungry Caterpillar* by Eric Carle

Balance

An effective way to describe the design feature of balance is to pass out picture books and have students discuss the cover designs. Remind students that authors/illustrators intentionally create and position images to capture the reader's attention. Most often images are balanced, although sometimes objects are placed in an asymmetrical way for emphasis. The focus when discussing this design feature is on point of view.

Questions to ask include:
- Where are the illustrations and text placed on the page, to what effect?
- What do you feel has the most visual weight or importance?
- Which design elements are most noticeable?

Favorite books: This activity can be done with the cover of any picture book. Using Caldecott award winners would be especially effective and interesting.

Appendix I

SIMPLE RUBRIC FOR WIKI POSTS

1. Your work must be quality (remember the *whole world* can see it).

2. Last names may not be included on work (*Internet safety issue*).

3. Remember to edit your work before posting.

Appendix J

GUIDELINES FOR COMMENTING ON WIKI WRITING

What is your role when you respond to a classmate on the wiki?

Checklist:

When I view and respond to someone's work I will . . .

	Support and validate their work.
	Encourage them as designers and writers.
	Offer helpful suggestions.
	Ask questions.
	Make connections with their work.
	Compliment their work (I like this piece because . . .).

Appendix K

SEARCH TOOLS FOR STUDENT RESEARCH

ALA Great Web Sites for Kids
http://www.ala.org/greatsites
High-quality content on sites rigorously screened
by the American Library Association

Ask Kids
http://www.ajkids.com/
Students ask questions and are directed to safe
Web pages that provide answers.

Fact Monster
http://www.factmonster.com/
Facts and information for children provided by
Information Please

Kids.gov
http://www.kids.gov/
From the U.S. Federal Citizen Information
Center, this directory provides links to
government-related kids' sites and other best
kid sites grouped by subject.

Google SafeSearch
http://onlinesafesearch.com/
Search kid-safe sites on a variety of subjects.

KidsClick!
http://www.kidsclick.org/
Five thousand Web sites in various categories
approved by librarians (reading levels
included)

KidsKonnect
http://www.kidskonnect.com/
Search a variety of kid-safe sites on many
subjects.

Kids' Search Tools
http://www.rcls.org/ksearch.htm
Search a variety of kid-safe search engines from a
single page.

OneKey
http://www.onekey.com/
Filtered database of kid sites partnered with
Google

**These two are favorites that require a
school or district subscription:**
netTrekker
http://www.nettrekker.com/us
Excellent connections to a variety of digital
resources (K–12)

Encyclopaedia Britannica Online
http://www.britannica.com/
Online encyclopedia provides thousands of
articles, biographies, videos, images, and Web
sites.

**For interest group investigations and
inquiries:**
Homelessness
http://www.endhomelessness.org

Consumerism
http://www.atg.wa.gov/teenconsumer

The Environment
http://www.pbskids.org/zoom/activities/action/
way04.html

Appendix L

ASSESSMENT MODEL FOR TWENTY-FIRST-CENTURY LEARNING

	PHASE 1 *Planning*	PHASE 2 *Involvement*	PHASE 3 *Evaluation of Learning*
Content	• What is your topic or subject? • What do you already know, and what questions will you ask? • How will you organize your learning?	• Is your information focused? • How are you gathering your information? • Are you using multiple resources?	• Is your assignment focused on topic? • Do you have detailed information? • Have you cited your resources?
Intent or Purpose	• What is the purpose or intention of this work? • How can this engagement make a difference in some way?	• Is the purpose clear? • Are multiple perspectives being considered?	• Does this artifact fulfill its purpose?
Audience	• Who is the audience for this work? • Who else might be interested?	• Is there awareness of audience? • Is it clear who the audience is or may be?	• Is it appropriate for the intended audience? • Who else might be interested?
Composition/Design	• What tools are needed? • Is the plan realistic? • Is the desired outcome clear? • What resources will be used? • How will this learning be shared?	• Are there a variety of tools and resources being used? • Are critical questions being asked? • Is the new vocabulary being applied?	• Did the tools and resources accomplish the desired effect? • Is the artifact focused and organized? • Does it include a variety of modalities?
Social Action	• Can you make real-life connections? • Is there an awareness of a need to make a difference?	• Are different outcomes being explored? • Are possibilities for social action being considered?	• Does the artifact make a difference/fulfill its purpose? • Is there potential for appropriate social action?
Reflection	• What were my thoughts/views when I started?	• What do I now know (understand, realize)? • What difference does this make to me? • How did this experience change my thinking/understanding?	• What new questions do I have from this experience? • How am I different? • How did this expand my understanding of multiliteracies to convey and communicate something meaningfully? • Did this make a difference for others and for myself?

Many Texts, Many Voices: Teaching Literacy and Social Justice to Young Learners in the Digital Age by Penny Silvers and Mary C. Shorey. Copyright © 2012. Stenhouse Publishers.

Appendix M

INTEREST GROUP ORGANIZER

Name: _____

1. Select a topic. _____

2. Who may be interested in your topic? _____

3. Who will you work with? _____

Have your topic approved by the teacher. _____

4. What resources do you need . . . books, Web sources? _____

_____

Gather resources…

5. Brainstorm questions to guide your research (attach these).

Share your questions with the teacher. _____

6. Write a **collaborative** report and discuss *why* your report is important.
   a. Discuss the design of your report with your group members.
   b. Share the writing.
   c. Pay attention to presentation.
      i. Did you capture the BIG ideas?
      ii. Is it edited?
      iii. Is it your best effort? A quality project?

Have your report monitored and checked by the teacher. _____

7. **Individual or group project(s).** These may be started after your group report is near completion.
   a. You may do more than one project, but you must have information and details gathered before you can put your information into a display.
   b. You need to pay attention to the design of your project—we will discuss design principles and ways to make your project work.

Have your project monitored and checked by the teacher. _____

Appendix N

STUDENT PLANNER CHECKLIST

☐ **Content**—Did I describe my topic, "tap" my prior knowledge, and design inquiry questions?

☐ **Intent**—Did I clearly explain my purpose?

☐ **Audience**—Did I identify my audience and expand it to include others who may be interested?

☐ **Composition/Design**—Did I select an effective way to communicate my learning (for ex., report, slideshow, video)?

☐ **Social Action**—How can I use my learning to make a difference for others and myself?

☐ **Reflection**—What am I thinking about now, and what new questions do I have? How is my thinking changed?

Note: This was adapted from Phase I of the Assessment Model.

Appendix O

INFOMERCIAL CHECKLIST

_____ Topic

_____ Information

_____ Message

_____ Action Plan

_____ Script draft

_____ Edit

_____ Final Draft

_____ Rehearse

_____ Videotape

_____ Edit in iMovie

_____ Publish and share

Appendix P

ASSESSMENT MODEL, PHASE 3: EVALUATION OF LEARNING

PHASE 3

	Evaluation of Learning	Student Reflection
Content	• Is your assignment focused on topic? • Do you have detailed information? • Have you cited your resources?	
Intent or Purpose	• Does this artifact fulfill its purpose?	
Audience	• Is it appropriate for the intended audience? • Who else might be interested?	
Composition/Design	• Did the tools and resources accomplish the desired effect? • Is the artifact focused and organized? • Does it include a variety of modalities?	
Social Action	• Does the artifact make a difference/fulfill its purpose? • Is there potential for appropriate social action?	
Reflection	• What new questions do I have from this experience? • How am I different? • How did this expand my understanding of multiliteracies to convey and communicate something meaningfully? • Did this make a difference for others and for myself?	

Additional comments:

Appendix Q

CRITICAL COMMUNITIES OF PRACTICE

() A *critical community of practice* emphasizes:
- "Who are we?"
  - We honor multiliteracies, prior experiences, cultures, and interests.
  - We respect all perspectives.
- "What are we interested in?"
  - We study the required content.
  - We focus on shared questions/inquiries.
  - We are responsive to individuals and the group.
  - We care about and support each other.

() Participation is the expectation.
- All forms of participation are valued.
- Collaboration is encouraged.
- The teacher is the lead learner.
- Students also share leadership or expert roles.

() Ownership in the learning process is shared.
- Students are advocates for their own and each other's needs.
  - Opportunities for support and enrichment are available.
  - Choices are part of all learning engagements.
  - Shared goal setting and reflective, responsive instruction is the norm.

An important difference in a critical community of practice is shared responsibility for meeting individual and group needs, and working together to accomplish the goals of the community, which often lead to some kind of social action.

Appendix R

TEXT SETS FOR THEMES: BIOGRAPHIES

Avi. 1997. *Finding Providence.* New York: HarperCollins.

Ballard, R. 1993. *Finding the Titanic.* New York: Scholastic.

Brenner, M. 1994. *Abe Lincoln's Hat.* New York: Random House.

Burleigh, R. 1997. *Flight: The Journey of Charles Lindbergh.* New York: Putnam and Grosset.

Engel, T. 1997. *We'll Never Forget You, Roberto Clemente.* New York: Scholastic.

Ferris, J. 1988. *Walking the Road to Freedom.* Minneapolis, MN: Lerner.

Gardeski, C. 2000. *Columbus Day.* New York: Scholastic.

Hass, E. 1995. *Read It to Believe It! Houdini's Last Trick.* New York: Random House Books for Young Readers.

Krull, K. 2000. *Wilma Unlimited.* Orlando: Harcourt.

————. 2010. *The Brothers Kennedy.* New York: Simon and Schuster.

Lasky, K. 1994. *The Librarian Who Measured the Earth.* New York: Little, Brown.

McGovern, A. 1978. *Shark Lady: True Adventures of Eugenie Clark.* New York: Scholastic.

Medearis, A. 1999. *Dare to Dream: Coretta Scott King and the Civil Rights Movement.* New York: Puffin.

Murphy, F. 2001. *Ben Franklin and the Magic Squares.* New York: Random House.

Reynolds, A. 2010. *Back of the Bus.* New York: Philomel.

Many Texts, Many Voices: Teaching Literacy and Social Justice to Young Learners in the Digital Age by Penny Silvers and Mary C. Shorey. Copyright © 2012. Stenhouse Publishers.

Appendix S

Many Texts, Many Voices: Teaching Literacy and Social Justice to Young Learners in the Digital Age by Penny Silvers and Mary C. Shorey. Copyright © 2012. Stenhouse Publishers.

TEXT SETS FOR THEMES: VISUAL LITERACY

Banyai, I. 1998. *Zoom*. New York: Penguin.

Browne, A. 1986. *Piggybook*. New York: Alfred A. Knopf.

———. 1998. *Voices in the Park*. New York: DK Publishing.

Bunting, E. 1994. *Smoky Night*. San Diego: Harcourt.

Carle, E. 1969. *The Very Hungry Caterpillar*. New York: Penguin.

Cherry, L. 1992. *A River Ran Wild*. Orlando: Harcourt.

Coleman, E. 1996. *White Socks Only*. Park Ridge, IL: Albert Whitman.

Fleischman, P. 1999. *Weslandia*. Somerville, MA: Candlewick.

Fox, M. 1985. *Wilfred Gordon MacDonald Partridge*. San Diego: Kane/Miller.

———. 1994. *Tough Boris*. San Diego: Harcourt Brace Jovanovich.

Hillman, B. 2008. *How Strong Is It?* New York: Scholastic.

Hoffman, M. 2002. *The Color of Home*. New York: Dial.

Johnson, C. 1955. *Harold and the Purple Crayon*. New York: HarperCollins.

Jonas, A. 1990. *Round Trip*. New York: Greenwillow.

Lorbiecki, M. 1998. *Sister Anne's Hands*. New York: Dial.

Macaulay, D. 1990. *Black and White*. Boston: Houghton Mifflin.

Munsch, R. 1983. *David's Father*. New York: Annick.

Myers, W. D. 1997. *Harlem: A Poem*. New York: Scholastic.

Pfister, M. 1992. *The Rainbow Fish*. New York: North-South.

Ringgold, F. 1991. *Tar Beach*. New York: Crown.

Say, A. 1993. *Grandfather's Journey*. Boston: Houghton Mifflin.

Shannon, D. 1998. *No, David!* New York: Scholastic.

Stewart, S. 2007. *The Gardener*. New York: Scholastic.

Weisner, D. 2001. *The Three Pigs*. New York: Clarion.

Willems, M. 2003. *Don't Let the Pigeon Drive the Bus!* New York: Hyperion.

Wood, A. 1987. *Heckedy Peg*. Orlando: Harcourt Brace.

Woodson, J. 2001. *The Other Side*. New York: Putnam.

Yolen, J. 1992. *Encounter*. New York: Harcourt, Brace, Jovanovich.

Appendix T

TEXT SETS FOR THEMES:
GENDER, IDENTITY, AND SELF-DISCOVERY

Bottner, B. 1992. *Bootsie Barker Bites.* New York: Putnam and Grosset.

Bridges, S. 2001. *Ruby's Wish.* San Francisco: Chronicle.

Browne, A. 1986. *Piggybook.* New York: Alfred A. Knopf.

————. 1998. *Voices in the Park.* New York: DK Publishing.

Choi, Y. 2003. *The Name Jar.* New York: Dell.

Cole, B. 1987. *Princess Smartypants.* New York: Penguin Putnam.

Corey, S. 2003. *Players in Pigtails.* New York: Scholastic.

DePaola, T. 1969. *Oliver Button Is a Sissy.* New York: Harcourt.

Desimini, L., and M. Mahurin. 2004. *My Beautiful Child.* New York: Blue Sky.

Fleming, C. 2006. *Lowji Discovers America.* New York: Atheneum.

Fox, Mem. 1988. *Koala Lou.* New York: Harcourt Brace.

————. 1994. *Tough Boris.* San Diego: Harcourt Brace Jovanovich.

————. 1996. *Feathers and Fools.* San Diego: Harcourt Brace.

Funke, C. 2001. *Princess Knight.* New York: Scholastic.

Henkes, K. 1991. *Chrysanthemum.* New York: Mulberry.

Hoffman, M. 1991. *Amazing Grace.* New York: Dial.

————. 2002. The *Color of Home.* New York: Dial.

Houston, G. 1992. *My Great-Aunt Arizona.* New York: HarperCollins.

Jackson, E. 1994. *Cinder Edna.* New York: William Morrow.

Lester, H. 1999. *Hooway for Wodney Wat.* Boston: Houghton Mifflin.

Martin, Bill, Jr. 2001. *Little Granny Quarterback.* Honesdale, PA: Boyds Mills.

Munsch, R. 2000. *The Paper Bag Princess.* Toronto: Annick.

Newman, L. 2000. *Heather Has Two Mommies.* New York: Scholastic.

Park, F., and G. Park. 2000. *The Royal Bee.* Honesdale, PA: Boyds Mills.

Pfister, M. 1992. *The Rainbow Fish.* New York: North-South.

Recorvits, H. 2003. *My Name Is Yoon.* New York: Farrar, Straus and Giroux.

Rosen, M. 1996. *This Is Our House.* Cambridge, MA: Candlewick.

Shannon, D. 1998. *No, David!* New York: Scholastic.

Spinelli, E. 1993. *Boy, Can He Dance!* New York: Four Winds.

Uegakui, C. 2003. *Suki's Kimono.* Toronto: Kids Can Press.

Wood, A. 1987. *Heckedy Peg.* Orlando: Harcourt Brace.

Yamate, S. 1992. *Ashok by Any Other Name.* Chicago: Polychrome.

Zolotow, C. 1972. *William's Doll.* New York: Harper and Row.

Appendix U

TEXT SETS FOR THEMES: ENDANGERED ANIMALS

Dillon, R. 2009. *Through Endangered Eyes: A Poetic Journey into the Wild.* Lakeville, MN: Windward.

Dobson, D., and J. Needham. 1997. *Can We Save Them? Endangered Species of North America.* Watertown, MA: Charlesbridge.

Gunzi, C. 2004. *The Best Book of Endangered and Extinct Animals.* Boston: Houghton Mifflin.

Hoare, B. 2010. *Eyewitness: Endangered Animals.* New York: DK Publishing.

Jenkins, S. 2006. *Almost Gone: The World's Rarest Animals.* New York: Collins.

Pasquali, E., and T. Macnaughton. 2010. *It's My World Too: Discover Endangered Animals and Their Habitats.* Oxford, UK: Lion.

Wright, A., and M. Peck. 1991. *Will We Miss Them?* Watertown, MA: Charlesbridge.

The Bald Eagle

Becker, J. 2002. *Returning Wildlife: The Bald Eagle.* San Diego: Kidhaven.

Gibbons, G. 1998. *Soaring with the Wind: The Bald Eagle.* New York: HarperCollins.

Minshull, E. 2002. *Eaglet's World.* Morton Grove, IL: Albert Whitman.

Priebe, M. 2000. *The Bald Eagle—Endangered No More* (Wildlife Winners). Norwalk, CT: Mindfull.

Stearns, C., and D. Aiken. 2002. *Quiet Please—Eaglets Growing.* Atglen, PA: Schiffer.

Appendix V

TEXT SETS FOR THEMES:
GENERATIONS, FAMILY, AND COMMUNITY

Bunting, E. 1989. *The Wednesday Surprise.* New York: Clarion.

———. 1991. *Fly Away Home.* New York: Clarion.

———. 1994. *Smoky Night.* San Diego: Harcourt Brace.

———. 2001. *The Wall.* New York: Clarion.

Carle, E. 1994. *The Very Hungry Caterpillar.* New York: Scholastic.

Cherry, L. 2007. *A River Ran Wild.* Orlando: Harcourt.

DePaola, T. 1975. *Strega Nona.* New York: Prentice Hall.

———. 1979. *Oliver Button Is a Sissy.* San Diego: Harcourt Brace Jovanovich.

———. 1988. *Now One Foot, Now the Other.* New York: Trumpet Club.

Fleischman, P. 1999. *Weslandia.* Somerville, MA: Candlewick.

Fox, M. 1985. *Wilfred Gordon MacDonald Partridge.* San Diego: Kane/Miller.

———. 1988. *Koala Lou.* San Diego: Harcourt Brace Jovanovich.

Garden, N. 2004. *Molly's Family.* New York: Farrar, Straus and Giroux.

Hillman, B. 2008. *How Strong Is It?* New York: Scholastic.

Johnson, C. 1998. *Harold and the Purple Crayon.* New York: HarperCollins.

Jonas, A. 1990. *Round Trip.* New York: Greenwillow.

McGovern, A. 1997. *The Lady in the Box.* New York: Turtle Books.

Mills, L. 1991. *The Rag Coat.* New York: Little, Brown.

Mora, Pat. 2009. *Gracias/Thanks.* New York: Lee and Low.

Munsch, R. 1983. *David's Father.* Toronto: Annick.

Norman, L. 2006. *My Feet Are Laughing.* New York: Farrar, Straus and Giroux.

Rylant, C. 1982. *When I Was Young in the Mountains.* New York: Dutton.

———. 1985. *The Relatives Came.* New York: Bradbury.

Say, A. 1993. *Grandfather's Journey.* Boston: Houghton Mifflin.

Stewart, S. (2007). *The Gardener.* New York: Square Fish.

Valasquez, E. 2010. *Grandma's Gift.* New York: Walker.

Willems, M. 2003. *Don't Let the Pigeon Drive the Bus!* New York: Hyperion.

Yolen, J. 1991. *All Those Secrets of the World.* Boston: Little, Brown.

———. 1992. *Encounter.* New York: Harcourt, Brace, Jovanovich.

Appendix W

TEXT SETS FOR THEMES: MULTICULTURAL EXPLORATIONS

Adler, D. 1993. *A Picture Book of Rosa Parks.* New York: Holiday House.

Anzaldua, G. 1995. *Friends from the Other Side/Amigios del otro lado.* San Francisco: Children's Book Press.

Bridges, R. 1999. *Through My Eyes.* New York: Scholastic

Bunting, E. 1994. *Smoky Night.* San Diego: Harcourt.

———. 1996. *Going Home.* New York: HarperCollins.

———. 1998. *So Far from the Sea.* New York: Clarion.

———. 2001. *Gleam and Glow.* San Diego: Harcourt.

Choi, Y. 2003. *The Name Jar.* New York: Knopf.

Cohen, B. 1983. *Molly's Pilgrim.* Boston: Lothrop.

Coleman, E. 1996. *White Socks Only.* Park Ridge, IL: Albert Whitman.

Coles, R. 1995. *The Story of Ruby Bridges.* New York: Scholastic.

Fleischman, P. 1997. *Seedfolks.* New York: HarperCollins.

Garland, S. 1977. *The Lotus Seed.* New York: Voyager.

Greenfield, E. 1978. *Honey, I Love, and Other Love Poems.* New York: Crowell.

Haskins, J. 1999. *Mr. Bojangles: The Biography of Bill Robinson.* New York: Welcome Rain.

Heide, F., and J. Gilland. 1990. *The Day of Ahmed's Secret.* New York: Scholastic.

Henkes, K. 1991. *Chrysanthemum.* New York: Greenwillow.

Hesse, K. 1993. *Letters from Rifka.* New York: Penguin.

Hoestlandt, J. 1993. *Star of Fear, Star of Hope.* New York: Scholastic.

Hoffman, M. 1991. *Amazing Grace.* New York: Dial.

———. 2002. *The Color of Home.* New York: Phyllis Fogelman.

Isadora, R. 1991. *Ben's Trumpet.* New York: Greenwillow.

Levine, E. 1995. *I Hate English!* New York: Scholastic.

Lorbiecki, M. 1998. *Sister Anne's Hands.* New York: Dial.

Maruki, T. 1980. *Hiroshima No Pica.* Boston: Lothrop.

Meyers, W. 1993. *Brown Angels.* New York: HarperCollins.

———. 1997. *Harlem.* New York: Scholastic.

———. 2011. *We Are America: A Tribute from the Heart.* New York: HarperCollins.

Miller, W. 1997. *Richard Wright and the Library Card.* New York: Lee and Low.

———. 1998. *The Bus Ride.* New York: Lee and Low.

Mochizuki, K. 1995. *Baseball Saved Us.* New York: Lee and Low.

Mora, P. 1997. *Tomas and the Library Lady.* New York: Alfred A. Knopf.

Polacco, P. 1994. *Pink and Say.* New York: Penguin Putnam.

Rappaport, D. 2001. *Martin's Big Words.* New York: Hyperion.

Recorvits, H. 2003. *My Name Is Yoon.* New York: Frances Foster.

Reynolds, A. 2005. *Chicks and Salsa.* New York: Bloomsbury U.S.A. Children's Books.

Ringgold, F. 1991. *Tar Beach.* New York: Crown.

———. 1992. *Aunt Harriet's Underground Railroad in the Sky.* New York: Crown.

———. 1999. *If a Bus Could Talk: The Story of Rosa Parks.* New York: Simon and Schuster.

Say, A. 1993. *Grandfather's Journey.* Boston: Houghton Mifflin.

Seurat, M. 1990. *Angel Child, Dragon Child.* New York: Scholastic.

Seuss, Dr. 1984. *The Butter Battle Book.* New York: Random House.

Shange, N. 1997. *White Wash.* New York: Walker.

Steptoe, J. 1997. *In Daddy's Arms I Am Tall: African Americans Celebrating Fathers.* New York: Lee and Low.

Wiles, D. 2001. *Freedom Summer.* New York: Atheneum.

Williams, V. 1982. *A Chair for My Mother.* New York: Harper Children's.

Winter, J. 1987. *Follow the Drinking Gourd.* New York: Alfred A. Knopf.

———. 2005. *The Librarian of Basra.* New York: Harcourt.

Woodson, J. 2001. *The Other Side.* New York: Putnam.

Yashima, T. 1955. *Crowboy.* New York: Viking.

Yolen, J. 1996. *Mother Earth, Father Sky.* Honesdale, PA: Wordsong.

Appendix X

TEXT SETS FOR THEMES: ENVIRONMENTAL STUDIES

Asch, F. 1994. *The Earth and I.* San Diego: Harcourt Brace.

Bergen, L., and B. Snyder. 2009. *Don't Throw That Away: A Lift-the-Flap Book About Recycling and Reusing.* New York: Little Simon.

Brown, R. 1991. *The World That Jack Built.* New York: Dutton Juvenile.

Cherry, L. 1990. *The Great Kapok Tree: A Tale of the Amazon Rain Forest.* New York: Harcourt.

Cooney, B. 1982. *Miss Rumphius.* New York: Scholastic.

Fleischman, P. 1999. *Weslandia.* Somerville, MA: Candlewick.

Gibbons, G. 1996. *Recycle! A Handbook for Kids.* New York: Little, Brown Books for Young Readers.

Green, J. 2005. *Why Should I Recycle?* Hauppauge, NY: Barron's Educational Series.

Guillain, C. 2008. *Reusing and Recycling (Help the Environment).* Mankato, MN: Heinemann-Raintree.

Harlow, R., and S. Morgan. 2002. *Garbage and Recycling.* New York: Macmillan.

Inches, A. 2009. *The Adventures of a Plastic Bottle.* New York: Little Simon.

Roca, N. 2007. *The Three R's: Reuse, Reduce, Recycle.* Hauppauge, NY: Barron's Educational Series.

Seuss, Dr. 1971. *The Lorax.* New York: Random House.

Showers, P. 1994. *Where Does the Garbage Go?* New York: Collins.

Van Allsburg, C. 1990. *Just a Dream.* Boston: Houghton Mifflin.

References

Professional References

Albers, P. 2007. *Finding the Artist Within*. Newark, DE: International Reading Association.

Anstey, M., and G. Bull. 2006. *Teaching and Learning Multiliteracies*. Newark, DE: International Reading Association.

Bloom, B. S. 1956. *Taxonomy of Educational Objectives, Handbook I: The Cognitive Domain*. New York: David McKay.

Bomer, R., and K. Bomer. 2001. *Reading and Writing for Social Action*. Portsmouth, NH: Heinemann.

Brennan, M. 2006. "Social Justice in a First-Grade Community of Practice." *School Talk* 12 (1): 5–6.

Cazden, C., B. Cope, N. Fairclough, J. Gee, M. Kalantzis, G. Kress, A. Luke, C. Luke, S. Michaels, and M. Nakata. 1996. "A Pedagogy of Multiliteracies: Designing Social Futures." *Harvard Educational Review* 66 (1): 60–93.

Comber, B. 2003. "Critical Literacy: What Does It Look Like in the Early Years?" In *Handbook of Early Childhood Literacy*, ed. N. Hall, J. Larson, and J. Marsh. Thousand Oaks, CA: Sage.

Cope, B., and M. Kalantzis. 2000. *Multiliteracies: Literacy Learning and the Design of Social Futures*. New York: Routledge.

Cowhey, M. 2006. *Black Ants and Buddhists: Thinking Critically and Teaching Differently in the Primary Grades*. Portland, ME: Stenhouse.

Crafton, L. 1991. *Whole Language: Getting Started, Moving Forward*. New York: Richard C. Owen.

Crafton, L., M. Brennan, and P. Silvers. 2007. "Critical Inquiry and Multiliteracies in a First-Grade Classroom." *Language Arts* 8 (6): 510–518.

Crafton, L., P. Silvers, and M. Brennan. 2008. "Creating a Critical Curriculum: Repositioning Art in the Early Childhood Classroom." In *Making Meaning: Constructing Multimodal Perspectives of Language, Literacy, and Learning Through the Arts*, ed. M. Narey. New York: Springer International.

Dewey, J. 1938. *Experience and Education.* New York: Collier Books.

Evans, J., ed. 2005. *Literacy Moves On: Popular Culture, New Technologies and Critical Literacy in the Elementary Classroom.* Portsmouth, NH: Heinemann.

Freire, P. 1998. *Teachers as Cultural Workers: Letters to Those Who Dare Teach.* Boulder, CO: Westview.

Gee, J. 2000. "Discourse and Sociocultural Studies in Reading." In *Handbook of Reading Research*, Vol. 3, ed. M. Kamil, P. Pearson, and R. Barr. Mahwah, NJ: Erlbaum.

Harste, J. 2007. "A Teacher's Story." In *Finding the Artist Within*, ed. P. Albers. Newark, DE: International Reading Association.

Harvey, S., and A. Goudvis. 2007. *Strategies That Work: Teaching Comprehension for Understanding and Engagement*, 2nd ed. Portland, ME: Stenhouse.

Kress, G. 2003. *Literacy in the New Media Age.* New York: Routledge.

Kucer, S. 2008. "What We Know About the Nature of Reading." In *What Research REALLY Says About Teaching and Learning to Read*, ed. S. Kucer. Urbana, IL: National Council of Teachers of English.

Leland, C., and J. Harste. 2004. "Critical Literacy: Enlarging the Space of the Possible." In *Literacy as Social Practice*, ed. V. Vasquez, K. Egawa, J. Harste, and R. Thompson. Urbana, IL: National Council of Teachers of English.

Leu, D., J. Castek, L. Henry, J. Coiro, and M. McMullan. 2004. "The Lessons That Children Teach Us: Integrating Children's Literature and the New Literacies of the Internet." *Reading Teacher* 57 (5): 496–503.

Lewison, M., A. Flint, and K. Van Sluys. 2002. "Taking On Critical Literacy: The Journey of Newcomers and Novices." *Language Arts* 79 (5): 382–392.

Lewison, M., C. Leland, and J. Harste. 2008. *Creating Critical Classrooms.* New York: Lawrence Erlbaum Associates.

Luke, A., and P. Freebody. 1999. "Further Notes on the Four Resources Model." *Reading Online.* http://www.readingonline.org/research/lukefreebody.html.

Marsh, J. 2005. *Popular Culture, New Media and Digital Literacy in Early Childhood.* New York: Routledge Falmer.

New London Group. 2000. "A Pedagogy of Multiliteracies." In *Multiliteracies: Literacy Learning and the Design of Social Futures*, ed. B. Cope and M. Kalantzis. New York: Routledge.

Ogle, D. 1986. "K-W-L: A Teaching Method That Develops Active Reading of Expository Text." *The Reading Teacher* 39: 564–570.

Owocki, G., and Y. Goodman. 2002. *Kidwatching: Documenting Children's Literacy Development.* Portsmouth, NH: Heinemann.

Riddle, J. 2009. *Engaging the Eye Generation: Visual Literacy Strategies for the K–3 Classroom.* Portland, ME: Stenhouse.

Siegel, M. 2006. "Rereading the Signs: Multimodal Transformations in the Field of Literacy Education." *Language Arts* 84 (1): 65–77.

Siegel, M., S. Kontovourki, S. Schmier, and G. Enriquez. 2008. "Literacy in Motion: A Case Study of a Shape-Shifting Kindergartner." *Language Arts* 86 (2): 89–98.

Vasquez, V. 2003. *Getting Beyond "I Like the Book": Creating Space for Critical Literacy in K–6 Classrooms.* Newark, DE: International Reading Association.

———. 2004. *Negotiating Critical Literacies with Young Children.* Mahwah, NJ: Lawrence Erlbaum.

Vasquez, V., K. Egawa, J. Harste, and R. Thompson, eds. 2004. *Literacy as Social Practice.* Urbana, IL: National Council of Teachers of English.

Vygotsky, L. 1978. *Mind in Society.* Cambridge, MA: Harvard University Press.

Wenger, E. 1998. *Communities of Practice: Learning, Meaning, and Identity.* New York: Cambridge University Press.

Wink, J. 2005. *Critical Pedagogy: Notes from the Real World.* Boston: Pearson Education.

Yelland, N., L. Lee, M. O'Rourke, and C. Harrison. 2008. *Rethinking Learning in Early Childhood Education.* New York: Open University Press.

References for Visual Literacy

Albers, P. 2007. *Finding the Artist Within.* Newark, DE: International Reading Association.

Berman, S. 1997. *Children's Social Consciousness and the Development of Social Responsibility.* Albany: State University of New York Press.

Burmark, L. 2002. *Visual Literacy: Learn to See, See to Learn.* Alexandria, VA: Association for Supervision and Curriculum Development.

Callow, J. 2003. "Talking About Visual Texts with Students." *Reading Online.* http://www.readingonline.org/articles/art_index.asp? HREF=callow/index.html.

———. 2006. "Images, Politics and Multiliteracies: Using a Visual Metalanguage." *Australian Journal of Language and Literacy* 2 (1): 7–23.

———. 2009. "Show Me: Principles for Assessing Students' Visual Literacy." *The Reading Teacher* 61 (8): 616–626.

Crafton, L. 1991. *Whole Language: Getting Started . . . Moving Forward.* New York: Richard C. Owen.

Crafton, L., M. Brennan, and P. Silvers. 2007. "Critical Inquiry and Multiliteracies in a First-Grade Classroom." *Language Arts* 8 (6): 510–518.

Dyson, A. 1993. *Social Worlds of Children.* New York: Teachers College Press.

———. 2003. "Popular Literacies and the 'All' Children: Rethinking Literacy Development for Contemporary Childhoods." *Language Arts* 81 (2): 100–109.

Moline, S. 2011. *I See What You Mean.* Portland, ME: Stenhouse.

Pantaleo, S. 2005. "Reading' Young Children's Visual Texts." *Early Childhood Research and Practice.* http://ecrp.uiuc.edu/v7n1/pantaleo.html.

———. 2007. "'How Could That Be?' Reading Banyai's Zoom and Re-zoom." *Language Arts* 84 (3): 222–233.

Unsworth, L. 2002. "Changing Dimensions of School Literacies." *Australian Journal of Language and Literacy* 25 (1): 62–76.

Vasquez, V. 2003. *Getting Beyond "I Like the Book": Creating Space for Critical Literacy in K–6 Classrooms.* Newark, DE: International Reading Association.

———. 2004. *Negotiating Critical Literacies with Young Children.* Mahwah, NJ: Lawrence Erlbaum Associates.

Williams, T. 2007. "'Reading' the Painting: Exploring Visual Literacy in the Primary Grades." *The Reading Teacher* 60 (7): 636–643.

References for Digital Literacy

Anstey, M., and G. Bull. 2006. *Teaching and Learning Multiliteracies.* Newark, DE: International Reading Association.

Evans, J., ed. 2005. *Literacy Moves On: Popular Culture, New Technologies and Critical Literacy in the Elementary Classroom.* Portsmouth, NH: Heinemann.

Gee, J. 2004. *Situated Language and Learning: A Critique of Traditional Schooling.* New York: Routledge.

Halliday, M. 1975. *Learning How to Mean.* New York: Elsevier.

Kress, G. 2003. *Literacy in the New Media Age.* New York: Routledge.

Labbo, L., and D. Reinking. 2003. "Computers and Early Literacy Education." In *Handbook of Early Literacy Research*, ed. S. Neuman and D. Dickinson. New York: Guilford.

Lankshear, C., and M. Knobel. 2003. *New Literacies: Changing Knowledge and Classroom Learning.* Philadelphia: Open University Press.

Leu, D., J. Castek, L. Henry, J. Coiro, and M. McMullan. 2004. "The Lessons That Children Teach Us: Integrating Children's Literature and the New Literacies of the Internet." *Reading Teacher* (5) 57: 496–503.

Lonestar. 2004. "Mr. Mom." *Let's Be Us Again.* BNA Entertainment.

Marsh, J. 2005. *Popular Culture, New Media and Digital Literacy in Early Childhood.* New York: Routledge Falmer.

New London Group. 2000. "A Pedagogy of Multiliteracies." In *Multiliteracies: Literacy Learning and the Design of Social Futures,* ed. B. Cope and M. Kalantzis. New York: Routledge.

Noddings, N. 1992. *The Challenge to Care in Schools.* New York: Teachers College Press.

Razfar, A., and E. Yang. 2010. "Digital, Hybrid, and Multilingual Literacies in Early Childhood." *Language Arts* 88 (2): 114–124.

Riddle, J. 2009. *Engaging the Eye Generation: Visual Literacy Strategies for the K–3 Classroom.* Portland, ME: Stenhouse.

Siegel, M. 2006. "Rereading the Signs: Multimodal Transformations in the Field of Literacy Education." *Language Arts* 84 (1): 65–77.

Vasquez, V. 2004. *Negotiating Critical Literacies with Young Children.* Mahwah, NJ: Lawrence Erlbaum.

———. 2010. "iPods, Puppy Dogs, and Podcasts: Imagining Literacy Instruction for the Twenty-First Century." *School Talk* 15 (2): 1–6.

Wohlwend, K. 2010. "A Is for Avatar: Young Children in Literacy 2.0 Worlds and Literacy 1.0 Schools." *Language Arts* 88 (2): 144–152.

Wollman-Bonilla, J. 2003. "E-mail as Genre: A Beginning Writer Learns the Conventions." *Language Arts* 81 (2): 126–134.

Index